# LEAVING
# WOMEN
# BEHIND
~

# LEAVING WOMEN BEHIND

~

## Modern Families, Outdated Laws

KIMBERLEY A. STRASSEL,
CELESTE COLGAN, AND
JOHN C. GOODMAN

ROWMAN & LITTLEFIELD PUBLISHERS, INC.
*Lanham • Boulder • New York • Toronto • Oxford*

THE NATIONAL CENTER FOR POLICY ANALYSIS
AND
THE MANHATTAN INSTITUTE

ROWMAN & LITTLEFIELD PUBLISHERS, INC.

Published in the United States of America
by Rowman & Littlefield Publishers, Inc.
A wholly owned subsidiary of The Rowman & Littlefield Publishing Group, Inc.
4501 Forbes Boulevard, Suite 200, Lanham, Maryland 20706
www.rowmanlittlefield.com

PO Box 317
Oxford
OX2 9RU, UK

Distributed by National Book Network

British Library Cataloguing in Publication Information Available

**Library of Congress Cataloging-in-Publication Data**

Colgan, Celeste.
    Leaving women behind : modern families, outdated laws /
    Kimberley A. Strassel, Celeste Colgan, and John C. Goodman.
        p. cm.
    Includes bibliographical references and index.
    ISBN 0-7425-4545-8 (cloth : alk. paper)
    1. Sex discrimination against women—United States. 2. Women—
Government policy—United States. 3. Women—Employment—
Social aspects—United States. 4. Women—United States—Social conditions—
20th century. 5. Women—United States—Economic conditions. 6. United
States—Social policy. 7. United States—Social conditions—1945-
I. Goodman, John C. II. Strassel, Kimberly A. III. Title.
HQ1237.5.U6C65 2006
305.42'0973—dc22                                                    2005021864

Printed in the United States of America

∞™ The paper used in this publication meets the minimum requirements of
American National Standard for Information Sciences—Permanence of Paper
for Printed Library Materials, ANSI/NISO Z39.48-1992.

# CONTENTS

~

# FOREWORD

## Senator Kay Bailey Hutchison

~

WORKING WOMEN today are paying a hefty price for being married and being mothers. It's about time to lower their burden. The National Center for Policy Analysis has written a lively, relevant book which zeroes in on the fact that the single most important economic and sociological change in our society in the last half century has been the entry of women into the labor market:

- Between 1950 and 2000, the labor force participation rate of women between 25 and 55 years of age more than doubled. Today, more than 75 percent of these women are in the labor market.
- Fewer than 12 percent of mothers with children under six were in the labor force in 1950. Today, more than 60 percent are working.

Despite these remarkable changes, and the major progress women have made in obtaining equality in the workplace, our public policy institutions have not kept pace. Underlying public policies—particularly tax policy and Social Security—were devised with one-income families in mind, inadvertently creating higher taxation and tough choices for those who work today outside the home.

Tax and labor laws are still designed to favor women who remain in the home and often penalize married women who enter the labor market. For example, the highest tax rates in our economy are mainly paid by women wage earners. The sad truth is that women earning only modest incomes sometimes pay taxes at rates that are twice those paid by such multimillionaires as Warren Buffett and Bill Gates. NCPA grabs these problems by the throat and suggests specific solutions to bring aging institutions into sync with the way women live their lives in the 21st century.

Practical solutions are contained in this book, including a fairer tax system for two-earner couples, perhaps one that allows both spouses to file completely separate tax returns. The authors describe a flexible benefit system that would give employees more choices, making it easier for a dual-earner couple to obtain higher wages rather than unneeded, duplicate benefits. They suggest flexibility in labor laws, making it possible for workers (especially parents with young children) to choose alternatives to the traditional 40-hour work week. And they discuss ways to make health and retirement benefits portable, so that people are not penalized when they switch jobs.

This book offers a compelling analysis of the changing demographics of American families today, considers the impact of often-unfair policies, and provides sound suggestions for addressing the problems.

# PREFACE

~

THE SINGLE most important economic and sociological change in our society in the past 60 years has been the entry of women into the labor market:

- Between 1950 and 2000 the labor force participation rate of women between 25 and 55 years of age more than doubled; today, more than 75 percent of these women are in the labor market.
- Less than 12 percent of mothers with children under six were in the labor force in 1950; today, more than 60 percent are working.

These changes have had a major impact on family life. For example:

- Since 1940, the proportion of working households that are one wage earner and a stay-at-home spouse has declined from two-thirds to less than one out of four (21 percent).
- Dual-earner families—with both spouses in the labor market—now constitute almost two-thirds of all married couples.

Despite these remarkable changes, our public policy institutions have not kept pace. Tax law, labor law, and a host of other institutions are still designed from top to bottom to favor women who remain in the home and are often unfair to married women who enter the labor market. The highest tax rates in our economy, for example, are mainly paid by women wage earners. In fact, women earning only modest incomes can pay taxes at twice the rates of those paid by such multimillionaires as Warren Buffett and Bill Gates. Consider that:

- Even if she earns only the minimum wage, a wife is taxed at her husband's tax rate. When all taxes and all costs are considered (including the cost of childcare and other services she was previously providing as a homemaker), a woman in a middle-income family can expect to keep only about 35 cents out of each dollar she earns.
- If the woman's husband dies prematurely, Social Security will provide a modest benefit as long as she stays home and takes care of children; but if she works, the combined effect of direct taxes plus loss of benefits will create a marginal tax rate of 87 percent—leaving her with only 13 cents out of each extra dollar she earns.
- Once the widow's children are grown, Social Security benefits will cease and she will be left to fend for herself; but if she previously responded to the system's antiwork incentives by remaining out of the labor market she will now have to enter the market without job skills.
- If the woman goes on welfare, she will confront a newly reformed system that is supposed to encourage work; however, when explicit taxes are combined with loss of benefits, her marginal tax rate will be about 79 percent—leaving her with only 21 cents out of each dollar of wage income.
- When the woman reaches retirement age she will once again qualify for Social Security benefits, but if she tries to supplement those benefits with wage income, special taxes on the elderly will make her marginal tax rate 64 percent—beyond a very modest level of income, she will get to keep only 36 cents out of each extra dollar she earns.

Of course, all the public policies that burden women can also in principle burden men. But because of the nature of work and family life, they are much less likely to do so. Here are some other examples:

- Both men and women workers pay the same unemployment insurance taxes, but because women are more likely to work part-time and because they voluntarily move in and out of the labor market more frequently (e.g., to raise children or care for a parent, etc.), they are less likely to receive any benefits in return for the taxes they pay.

- Because Social Security taxes are levied on all earnings until capped at a high-income level, dual-earner households generally pay considerably more in taxes than single-earner households, but they will get only a minimal increase in Social Security benefits.
- Because women live longer than men, they will be more burdened by the income taxes paid on Social Security benefits, which will cause many middle-income seniors to forfeit more than half of their private pension income and IRA withdrawals.

Women are adversely affected by public policies in other ways. In contrast to some other developed countries, the United States encourages employers rather than government to provide such benefits as health insurance and pensions. Our private employee benefits system is not the result of free market forces, however. Instead, it has been shaped and molded by federal law designed to accommodate a full-time worker with a stay-at-home spouse and penalize any other arrangement. For example:

- Because they are more likely to work part-time, women are less likely to qualify for employer-provided benefits.
- Because they move from job to job and in and out of the labor market more frequently than men, women are more likely to be burdened by employee benefit programs that penalize job switching (e.g., lack of vesting in a pension plan).
- And when people acquire health insurance and save for retirement on their own (not through an employer), the tax system is far less generous.

Couples with two full-time working adults are disadvantaged in other ways by the current system. They often find that they must accept unnecessary, duplicate sets of employee benefits, say, because the wife is unable to opt for higher wages if she forgoes health insurance from her own employer when she is already covered on her husband's employer's plan.

Many changes are needed to bring aging institutions into sync with the way people live in the 21st century. Here are a few suggestions:

- We need a fairer tax system for two-earner couples, perhaps one that allows both spouses to file completely separate tax returns.
- We need a flexible employee benefit system that gives employees more choices, making it easier for dual-earner couples to obtain higher wages rather than unneeded, duplicate benefits and for part-time workers to accept lower wages in return for more valuable health and retirement benefits.
- We need flexibility in labor law, making it easier for workers (especially parents with young children) to choose alternatives to the traditional 40-hour workweek.
- We need to replace the arbitrary limits on retirement savings contributions with a system that is fairer to women who move in and out of the workplace.
- We need a fairer system for providing tax relief for health insurance—especially for single parents who leave the workforce for extended periods of time.
- We need to find ways to make health and retirement benefits portable—so that people are not penalized when they switch jobs.
- We need a completely new approach to the treatment of spouses under Social Security; earnings sharing (where payroll tax contributions are divided like community property) could easily be applied to any new system of personal retirement accounts.
- We should consider abolishing the earnings penalty for those receiving Social Security survivor's benefits.

Unlike many other writings on "women's issues," this book does not assume that in order for some people to be successful we must limit the freedom or raise the taxes of others. Nor are we promoting social or cultural outcomes. Instead, we assume that women in our society are capable of making choices that are right for them and are perfectly capable of living productive, satisfying lives, provided that misguided public policies do not hold them back.

┌─────────┐
│    1    │
│    ~    │
└─────────┘

# INTRODUCTION

READERS OF THIS book might remember the 1998 movie *Pleasantville*. It opens with David, a lonely teen living in the fantasy twilight of the 20th century. David is disillusioned with his modern world. His divorced mother never ceases squabbling with his deadbeat dad, and the teachers in his gigantic, soulless high school never tire of warning him that it's a dangerous world. So he spends his evenings in front of the television watching reruns of a 1950s sitcom called *Pleasantville*, until one day he is magically sucked into the TV show.

And Pleasantville is . . . very pleasant. David lands in the house of George and Betty Parker, who are everything we'd expect 1950s, middle-class Americans to be. George goes to work every morning to the same job he always has, and returns home every evening to cheerfully announce: "Honey, I'm home." Betty cooks and cleans and still has time to whip up a cold martini for George every night. She's always available for their two children, Bud and Mary Sue, who attend the town's local high school—where they know all their classmates and learn everything they need to know.

People in Pleasantville don't get divorced, they wouldn't dream of claiming welfare, and nobody has doctor bills their HMOs won't pay. We get the feeling that George and Betty will continue merrily along in this fashion until one day, say a year or two after George retires, they both peacefully pass away.

The point of this book isn't to judge which version of America is better—1950s Pleasantville or the more complicated present. The point is to show that while most of America is living in David's modern, complicated world, some of our most important public policies assume we are living in Pleasantville. From taxes to Social Security to employee benefits law, we are coping with institutions designed for families who live and work just like the Parkers. This has a profound impact on our entire society, but it has particularly onerous consequences for women.

The single most important economic and sociological change in our society in the past 60 years has been the entry of women into the labor market. Between 1950 and 2000, the labor force participation of women between the ages of 25 and 55 more than doubled. Today, more than 75 percent of women in this age group have traded in Betty Parker's feather duster for a time card, regardless of whether they have children. More than 60 percent of women with children under the age of six are working for wages.

Yet while women are galloping headlong into change, our public policies stand frozen in time. Tax law, labor law, and many other major government institutions are still designed to accommodate women who remain in the home, often at the expense of the woman who packs a briefcase. Married working women pay higher taxes because they fall into their husband's typically higher bracket; they are discriminated against when it comes to employee benefits because of archaic workplace rules; and they face an insecure retirement because of outdated entitlement programs geared toward one-earner, stay-together couples.

Many of the difficulties described in this book apply equally to the opposite sex: Husbands not only share the burdens of their wives, but growing numbers of *men* play the role of stay-at-home spouse. Still, while things have changed, they haven't changed entirely. Women not only find themselves going toe-to-toe with outdated policies, in the majority of cases they are still primarily responsible for arranging family life and childcare.

## 10 ASSUMPTIONS ABOUT AMERICA

Considering when most of our major institutions were drawn up, it's no wonder they're running on only a few cylinders. Our schools evolved at a time when Americans lived in rural communities or close-knit neighborhoods, and teachers often boarded with local parents. Social Security got rolling in the 1930s when a lot of the country was still marveling at electricity and running water. The income tax picked up speed in the 1940s at a time when we were at war. Medicare started in 1965, before we'd even put a man on the moon. Despite a few tweaks or updates along the way, most of these institutions still look much as they did when our parents and grandparents designed them.

In fairness, these institutions and the laws governing them were created by well-intentioned people with an earnest desire to meet basic human needs. And, for much of the 20th century, these policies served society well. It just so happens that most of the assumptions about work and family life upon which they were built have gone the way of the Model T Ford.

Imagine, for a moment, the architects of today's institutions sitting down to craft their plans. Before they could come up with a program to help America with retirement benefits or health care or deal with any other problem they had to decide what America *was*. Had they drawn up a list—call it "10 Assumptions about America"—it would have run something like this:

1. America is a nation of traditional, married families where a husband goes out to collect a paycheck and a wife goes out to collect the groceries and the children from school.
2. The husband will faithfully work for only one employer, probably for his entire adult life.
3. This husband will work a full, 40-hour week, and he'll have no need for temporary or part-time jobs.
4. The wife, since she doesn't work outside the home, will scoff at the notion of childcare.
5. The family will obtain employee benefits, such as health insurance or a pension, through the husband's lifelong employer.

6. Couples will not get divorced.
7. Couples will not retire, or at least not for very long, since most will not live past the age of 65.
8. Families will have lots of children, who will ultimately work and pay for the older generation's retirement benefits.
9. These children will attend schools where quality is maintained by elected citizens of high standing in the community and involved families.
10. Those in need of welfare assistance will be mainly widows and orphans.

These "10 Assumptions About America" are not a bad description of the country for most of the past century. In 1940, two-thirds of households had one person who went to work and one person who stayed home. Similarly, in 1950, fewer than 12 percent of mothers with children under the age of six were in the labor force.

Obviously, things have changed. If you think for a moment about your own family or friends, chances are you'll struggle to come up with one who fits even most of the assumptions on the list. What this means in practical terms is that very few Americans today are getting from our institutions what those institutions were originally designed to supply. And since many of the 10 assumptions have been undermined by the changing role of women, it is women who are most disadvantaged by outdated institutions and ideas.

This book will deal with 10 areas of work and family life that are particularly challenging to married couples in general and women in particular. Let's conduct a brief review.

## THE FIRST DAY ON THE (INFLEXIBLE) JOB

Most of us spend our early years fretting about *getting* a job. It may not be until the first day on the job that we realize a bigger problem is *how* we are allowed to work. Women in particular run up against a huge number of obstacles that stem from laws governing the workplace. Most of these regulations were drafted in the 1930s, in some cases to protect employees from abusive employers. Today, they've become abusive in and of themselves.

Consider, for example, the lack of workplace flexibility. Labor laws written years ago require that full-time hourly workers be paid time and a half if they work longer than 40 hours a week. For the most part, workers who want to take occasional time away from their jobs must either take annual leave, or leave without pay. In neither case are they allowed to store up hours one week and work fewer hours the next. These rules are particularly bizarre given that we live in a world where people no longer need to be chained to a desk for precisely eight hours every day— especially in light of cellular phones, Internet connections, mobile offices, and part-time consulting work. Women, who are often tasked with juggling childcare and other family responsibilities, find these strictures particularly burdensome.

Outmoded workplace rules also run roughshod over employee benefits programs. The "10 Assumptions" crowd lived in a world where men were expected to work 40-hour weeks and bring home both the bacon and the benefits. Part-time workers, it was assumed, had no need for perks. But today one-fourth of all women work in part-time jobs, and they don't always have a spouse to procure health insurance or a pension for them.

Current law discourages companies from offering part-time workers employee benefits. Millions of couples would jump at the chance if both spouses could work 20–30 hours a week and still get health insurance and a pension. But in today's labor market, they are usually out of luck. And there is no flexibility within the benefits system: If a wife *is* offered a benefit that happens to duplicate her husband's benefit in some other job, she won't be able to get higher wages in lieu of unneeded perks.

Aside from work rules, women find themselves disadvantaged by the type of work they do. Smaller companies today employ more than half of all the nation's workers, and women gravitate toward many of the fields in which small companies are active. But while larger companies often offer a wide range of benefits, small companies frequently do not. And when people who work part-time or for small companies buy their own health insurance they get little if any tax relief. If they attempt to save for retirement on their own, the system is not much better.

Women who go in and out of the workforce or work part-time, say, as a result of children, are also penalized in other ways. Our unemployment compensation system, established in 1935, requires people who work part-time to pay the same unemployment tax as full-time workers. But it is much harder for part-timers to qualify for unemployment benefits, and they are only one-fourth as likely to see any money back from their pay-in. Even among full-time workers, women receive no benefits if they leave the labor market to raise children or care for a parent. They also get no help once they reenter the market to search for a job.

## Bringing Up Baby

Even women with small children today are likely to work. And while both husband and wife have a stake in overcoming the problems, it is usually the mother who has the primary job of finding, retaining, and paying for suitable childcare.

Her first shock will be childcare expenses, and the government isn't much help. Our tax law has a credit for childcare expenses, but it is well below most families' actual expenses. Mothers who are fortunate enough to have a relative, friend, or another family member help them out with informal care find that there is no way for them to claim any tax relief.

Employee benefits law on childcare policy is also arbitrary. Women who work for large employers and set up flexible spending accounts can funnel pretax wages to purchase childcare services. But among small businesses this opportunity is rare and the option is nonexistent for women on their own. Large companies are able to deduct unlimited spending on daycare programs for their employees. But given the bureaucratic red tape and costs of setting up and running these programs, small businesses usually aren't able to offer the same deal.

Red tape is crisscrossed over every speck of the childcare industry. While women complain of a shortage of affordable daycare facilities, there are probably thousands of private individuals, particularly women, who would love to fill the gap with childcare facilities out of their homes. But who is going to venture into the field when federal, state, and local laws regulate the number of square feet of playing space per child, the hours of operation, and virtually all other aspects of child-care? As one woman who'd considered (but ultimately decided against) a home-based daycare facility told us: "If you think three-year-olds are a handful, just try dealing with the state bodies that tell you how to watch three-year-olds."

## THE TAXWOMAN COMETH

Surely, you say, the payoff of navigating these thorny workplace rules and childcare expenses is the paycheck at the end of the week? Sadly, many women run the obstacle course only to find they are bringing home a meager percentage of what they earn. That's partly because for more than 50 years our income tax system has rewarded the stay-at-home mom and penalized the one who works for wages.

Granted, few people like taxes. But taxes hit women in particularly onerous ways. For one thing, the tax law lumps wives' earnings in with their husbands'. In two-earner families, that means the spouse who earns less will still be in the other's higher tax bracket. Since women are likely to earn less than men, married women who work are taxed at rates much higher than single women who earn the same wage. In fact, working wives at all income levels tend to take home less than half of what they earn. In some cases, the combined salaries of two earners push them into an entirely new and higher tax bracket, in which they pay more taxes than if they were single. This is the "marriage penalty," and ironically it is most severe at the top and bottom of the income ladder. Perversely, it encourages high-income women not to work at all and low-income women not to marry.

Taxes aren't the only thing that eats away at a woman's paycheck. Usually a stay-at-home wife is providing essential services to the family: cooking, laundering, housekeeping, and childcare. If she decides to enter the labor market, the couple will probably have to pay someone else for some of these same tasks (unless she is Wonder Woman). Factoring in these costs, we judge that the typical middle-class housewife can expect to net as little as one-third of what she earns when she enters the labor market.

## HEALTH CARE, ON LIFE SUPPORT

Families may share the responsibilities of home life, but the biggest decisions (left over from the days of Betty Parker) still typically fall to women—especially in the realm of health care. Women today are still responsible for 60 percent of spending in the medical marketplace, frequently making decisions for their children as well as themselves.

When women enter the health care system, they are likely to rely on health insurance provided by an employer—the result of our 60-year-old system of employer-based health insurance. It is a system under which employers choose health care plans for employees and their families, and employees have little control and few choices. On that score, little has changed since the end of World War II.

Yet while the system of getting health care through an employer hasn't changed, the type of health care you get most certainly has. When employer-based health insurance first emerged, it was predominantly "fee for service." Employees could choose to see virtually any doctor and they were reimbursed by the company's insurance plan for whatever test or procedure the doctor ordered. If an employee did change jobs, there was no reason to change doctors, since the new employer's plan was also likely to operate the same way.

Today things are different. In a managed care world, the doctors you are able to see are likely to be limited to those in your employer's health plan network. Even if you have the right to go out of network, the out-of-pocket costs are likely to be higher. These restrictions affect men as well as women. But they affect women more. Not only do women tend to use doctors more frequently than men, the health care system is less likely to treat them appropriately for conditions that range from chronic pain to heart disease. So women have more at stake when they search for a doctor.

Under managed care, a job change almost always means you have to change health plans too. And that often means you have to change doctors as well. So the system works best for people who stick with one company for their entire working lives. It works least well in a mobile labor market where people move from job to job frequently. Disruptions may also occur even if you don't change jobs. Most employer contracts with health insurance plans last only 12 months; and at the end of the year, it is the employer's option to switch. Either way, the result is the same for women and their physicians, whether pediatrician or gynecologist—a break in the continuity of care.

In today's system, women rarely have the option to choose a health plan that is right for them. Some people might be willing to pay more out-of-pocket expenses in return for the right to use any physician. Others might limit their range of doctors in return for lower costs. Younger, healthier couples may place a higher value on preventive care than chronic care. Older employees may want a plan that offers more in prescription drug benefits, but less of something else. But in today's system, employers are forced to offer one-size-fits-all programs that give everybody a little of something and nobody exactly what he or she needs.

So why don't people have portable health insurance they can carry from job to job? Standing in the way of this sensible idea is outdated tax law, which favors insurance that is provided by an employer and penalizes people who purchase their own. Every dollar your company pays in insurance premiums is a dollar that you don't have to pay taxes on. But if your employer gives you that same money to purchase your own insurance, taxes come out first and you have to buy the insurance with what's left over. Even if the employer buys insurance for you, if it's the personal and portable kind it has to be purchased with after-tax dollars.

We're stuck with a system that doesn't work well because that's the system the government subsidizes.

## A Failing Grade for Schools

At least in health care, women may have *some* options. When it comes to another major family job—finding a quality school for their children—they may have no choices whatsoever. Our schools were based on the century-old assumption that our system of education would be used by intact families who exerted control. In the old days, if Susie didn't care to learn her times tables, her teacher sent for her parents. And if Susie's instructor wasn't bothering to *teach* Susie her times tables, her parents went to the local school board and demanded the teacher be fired.

In modern times parents find themselves swept into vast urban school districts that rarely fire anyone (certainly not for incompetence) and where control is exercised more by local teachers' unions than by parents in the neighborhood. Women, who continue to make a majority of the decisions about selecting and monitoring their children's education, face two major problems: getting information about the quality of schools, and more importantly, getting their children into schools that are good.

Until recently, most public schools refused to release information about student scores on SAT tests and other state and national exams. Over time, that's changed, and a law passed by Congress a few years back requires uniform testing in all 50 states. Yet even this uniform testing can be misleading or incomplete, and parents still lack the kind of information that will give them a real picture about what different schools can do for their children.

But say a mother does manage to get good information about nearby schools. What does it matter if she has no choice over where she can send her child? For many parents, the only way to ensure that a child learns how to read or write is to have enough money to move into an expensive house in an expensive neighborhood. Granted, the advent of magnet and charter schools is giving parents some options within the public system, and in a few places vouchers allow them to explore the private school arena. But state and federal laws will need to change dramatically before parents begin to have real control over how their own children learn.

## THE SCRAMBLED NEST EGG

None of us wants to get old, but aging is of particular concern for women (and not just because they don't like wrinkles). Since women tend to live longer, they need more funds for retirement. Their longer lives also mean they are more likely to be alone near the end of their retirement years. Yet far too many elderly women find they are struggling to make ends meet with fewer resources than they really need.

Government seems to work overtime to discourage women from saving and investing during their younger years. Our defined-benefit pension system (in which employees are promised a specific dollar benefit during retirement) evolved more than six decades ago. Employees accumulate pension benefits based on years of service to the company, and those who remain with one company throughout their work life can typically retire with a pension equal to 60 percent or more of final pay. This is the system designed for George Parker and was never meant for a dynamic workforce. The defined benefit system penalizes those who change jobs. Women who drop in and out of the labor market (to raise children or care for an ailing parent) are treated severely under this system. And women who have part-time jobs often do not have access to pension benefits at all.

Most employers have switched over to more modern, defined contribution plans (in which employees get whatever their account grows to by the time of retirement). A popular example is the 401(k) plan, in which a percentage of employee contributions are sometimes matched by employers, and employees make their own investment decisions. Employees with 401(k) plans are theoretically able to move the funds with them if they change jobs. Even so, they still face "vesting" requirements, under which they obtain full rights to the funds in their account only if they stay on the job long enough. The woman who dutifully contributes to her 401(k), but then unexpectedly leaves the workforce to raise a child, may find that she forfeits expected savings.

There are also arbitrary government limits on how much people can contribute. Depending on the plan, a person's income, and any number of other factors, some people are allowed to put as much as $40,000 into a tax-deferred savings plan in one year, while others may be limited to an annual $3,500 contribution to an IRA. These rules apply to men as well as women, but women are more likely to be subject to the arbitrary limits. Another problem: women need to do a lot of saving in the years they work, to offset the times they aren't employed.

## SOCIAL INSECURITY

If all this sounds discouraging, consider what a woman has to look forward to if she doesn't save: total reliance on Social Security. This federal retirement program gets the hands-down prize for the biggest number of outdated assumptions, most of which have important consequences for women.

When the program was established, with its retirement age of 65, life expectancy in the United States was less than 65. So the framers of the program expected most of us to die before we ever became eligible to collect a dime. Today, however, one in every eight Americans is over age 65, and most of them are women.

The framers also had a particular kind of family in mind: a family with one wage earner and a stay-at-home spouse. Social Security is generous to women who never work. Wives, for instance, are entitled to pension benefits equal to half their husband's benefit. And if he dies first, she gets 100 percent of his benefits for the rest of her life. But many women who work and pay devotedly into the system over the years receive few, if any, extra Social Security benefits in return for all the taxes they paid.

The one-earner family notion gets even more knotty if a woman's husband dies prematurely. Social Security survivor benefits encourage the surviving spouse to remain in the home with children the entire time she receives the benefits. In fact, the woman has two unsavory options: She can dare to work, and get hit with a severe penalty in the form of reduced benefits. Or she can stay home and survive off a government paycheck until the day her youngest child hits 16—at which time the checks stop. But at that point she will enter the labor market at mid-career with no training, no experience, and 20 years to go until she herself is able to retire.

Finally, Social Security framers must have assumed that divorce would be a rarity, for they certainly gave very little thought to it. Under the rules, a marriage must last 10 years before a wife is entitled to any benefits based on her husband's contributions. This is both arbitrary (is the wife who lasted nine years and eleven months any less deserving than one who made it to 10 years?) and out of step with modern times. Half of all marriages today end in divorce, and the average divorce takes place in just seven years!

## THE NOT-SO-GOLDEN YEARS

In modern times, we have come to think that retirement should be a normal, natural part of life. Not all people will choose to cease working at the same age. Some will work into their 70s and 80s, while others will retire in their 50s. The idea that everyone should face a completely different world the minute he or she turns 65 is out of step with the way most Americans want to live their lives.

Yet a number of important public policies segregate people who are 65 and older and treat them differently. For example, until very recently, Social Security severely penalized anyone who worked beyond the age of 65. We also segregate our retirees in other ways, shunting them off into a different tax system and a different health care system.

Even if people manage to clear the high hurdles of saving during their working years, they may be shocked when they learn how little of what they have saved they get to keep. Social Security's saving grace is that it provides a floor for many low-income seniors—meager though that floor is. But when middle-income seniors who saved their whole lives withdraw their retirement funds, they face some of the highest tax rates in the nation—higher, for example, than what most millionaires pay. The Social Security benefits tax sounds like a tax on Social Security. In reality, it is a tax on all other income, including pension checks and IRA withdrawals. Even for moderate-income seniors, government can take more than half of their IRA income.

Most seniors also land in an entirely new health care program at age 65, whether working or retired, healthy or sick. Medicare, insulated from reforms undergone by the rest of the health care system, has become inferior to the health insurance most of the rest of the nation has. Seniors are the only members of our society who must buy a second health plan to fill in the gaps in their primary health plan. Even with two plans, most seniors do not typically have coverage they need for the prescription drugs and end up paying significant out-of-pocket expenses.

## It Can Only Get Worse . . .

In general, government-run senior programs aren't much to look forward to. And the cherry on top of this unappetizing cake is that they are set to get much worse. Very soon, Social Security and Medicare combined will begin paying out more in benefits than they receive in payroll taxes. And from that point on, the financial problems will get worse—day by day, month by month, year by year, indefinitely into the future.

Part of the problem once again rests in antiquated notions about how people are going to live their lives. Back in the days when women stayed at home, they tended to have more children. The crafters of elderly entitlement programs assumed that the U.S. population would continue to grow at a brisk rate and that there would always be a lot of young 'uns to pay for the older folk. But with growing numbers of women in the workplace, fertility rates have dropped so low that we are no longer even replacing our population, much less adding to its long-term growth. Put simply, we're going to run out of people to work and pay taxes.

Both Medicare and Social Security are "pay-as-you-go" programs. Contrary to what a lot of voters think (and what a lot of politicians suggest), there is no money stashed away for future benefits. Every payroll tax dollar that lands in Washington today is immediately spent on retirement benefits, snatched by politicians for other programs, or sent to pay down the national debt. Unless and until our elderly entitlement programs are put on surer footing, our future will consist of fewer benefits for retirees, higher taxes for workers, or both.

## Fare Thee Well to Old-Fashioned Welfare

Among all this doom and gloom there is a bright spot. In 1995, the federal government proved that with a little creative thinking and a lot of gumption, it could tackle at least one of the national institutions so desperately out of sync with modern life. The result was welfare reform.

Until the last decade of the 20th century, the federal government's approach to welfare was as outdated as the other institutions described here. It assumed that single motherhood would be rare and temporary and that if it did occur a young girl's extended family would be around to help. Up until (ironically enough) the time that Lyndon Johnson began his War on Poverty in 1965, this was largely true.

But sometime in the 1960s, Americans began to worry less about the social stigma of having children out of wedlock or collecting a welfare check. Aid, in the meantime, became so generous that millions of women would ultimately be lured into a state of dependency. By 1992, federal and state programs had spent $5 trillion on Johnson's "War," and all they had to show for it was a higher poverty rate than when the battle was first joined.

This was partly because the program had evolved in such a way that welfare recipients faced draconian penalties if they tried to escape—in the form of high taxes and a loss of benefits. To make matters worse, the welfare bureaucracy had become so inept that it paid large chunks of money to people who weren't really "poor." Along the way, the system crowded out private charities that otherwise might have been better equipped to cope with individual circumstances and to help people get back to work.

Welfare reform changed this depressing picture. States are now using both carrots and sticks to motivate people to say goodbye to welfare forever. Local governments have the ability to use their funds in ways that will get people employed—job training, substance abuse treatment, childcare—rather than pay them not to work. There is also the threat to cut off aid to those who don't make honest efforts to change their own circumstances. Much remains to be done, primarily in giving states (and even individual taxpayers) more flexibility and more options. But a look at declining welfare roles, even in the recent economic downturn, shows that government, if it wants to, is capable of modernizing even the most ingrained public institutions.

## WHAT'S TO BE DONE?

The good news is that these problems have solutions. Scholars and policy wonks and think tanks have come up with any number of bright and innovative ways to update our outdated laws and institutions. The bad news is that welfare reforms don't happen every day. Convincing Washington politicians to tinker with, much less entirely reform, large institutions may prove harder than coaching the Chicago Cubs to a World Series title.

But tackle reform they must if some of America's most important institutions are going to survive in the 21st century. Women in particular need to start demanding changes from their elected representatives. Their to-do list should run something like this:

> Working couples in general and female workers in particular need a new set of rules governing the workplace. They should have the ability to adjust their work hours in order to meet family needs as well as employer needs. They should be able to trade off unneeded perks for

higher wages and needed benefits. They should be able to choose non-traditional hours of work without losing health insurance and pension benefits. And even when employers pay health insurance premiums and contribute to retirement plans, those benefits should be personal and portable—traveling with employees as they go from job to job.

We won't get these changes by having government order everyone around. To the contrary, government should get out of the way. Employers and employees across the country are perfectly capable of making mutually beneficial adjustments if we simply untie their hands.

In other areas, government cannot get out of the way because the problem is government itself. The solutions here involve empowering people, giving them more choices and making government less intrusive.

For example, virtually all our social insurance programs are in need of radical reform, from unemployment compensation to Social Security. The overhaul will be complete when they no longer discriminate against working women. Similarly, our income tax system should stop penalizing marriage; and among married couples, it should stop penalizing wives who work. The goal should be a tax system that treats women fairly and as workers in their own right, rather than as a marital unit.

The tax system should also recognize the myriad ways (all of them valid) in which working mothers obtain childcare. It should stop ignoring the fact that people who move in and out of the labor market need to be able to save more for retirement during the periods when they are earning an income. And the tax system should recognize that people who must purchase health insurance on their own or save for their own retirement need tax relief as much or more than those who obtain these benefits through an employer.

Whenever possible, the empowerment of individuals is preferable to mindless regulation. People are usually able to discern their own self-interest much better than government employees. And people care more about themselves than government employees do. Parents, for example, need more choices in choosing schools and daycare. And women in particular need more opportunity to exert direct control over their own health care dollars.

Everyone wants to look forward to a safe and secure retirement. This means we need Social Security and Medicare programs that aren't dependent on later generations, but allow each generation of workers to save and pay its own way. Clearly, we need a tax system that doesn't discriminate against senior citizens and a private health care system that doesn't exclude those over the age of 65.

What follows in this book is a critical discussion of the difficulties men and women face in the 21st century, along with potential solutions to those problems. The goal of this book isn't to paint women as victims; they have proved over the past century that, despite barriers, they have reinvented Betty Parker into a vibrant modern American woman. The goal of this book, then, is to show that with a bit of clear thinking and some much needed reform the future potential for women is boundless.

## FOCUS ON THE FEDS

Readers will notice that most of the problems and reforms we discuss in the ensuing pages are directed at the federal government. This is for the simple reason that federal laws and institutions have lagged far behind the rest of the nation in coming to grips with the new role women play in society.

Certainly, the entry of millions of women into the workforce has brought about wrenching economic and sociological change that hasn't been easy to absorb. But America is a vibrant place, and many institutions have made huge strides in the face of this revolution. State and local laws, societal attitudes, and the business community have all adapted in remarkable ways.

Consider everyday family life. Fifty years ago, men were "breadwinners" and women were "housewives" and the discussion usually stopped there. Today, marriage and motherhood are viewed as choices women make. The word "housewife" has all but vanished from modern lingo, replaced by "stay-at-home moms" who more likely than not will storm back into the labor force once their children are old enough to be managed alongside their jobs.

The workplace they enter has also taken on a whole new form. In the strong American economy of the late 20th century, businesses found themselves competing for talented and experienced employees like never before and recruited women by the droves. A young woman who graduates from college today will vie for the best jobs with her male peers. This new generation of women workers flood into every industry, and those who don't take time out to have children will continue to command the same salaries as men. Moreover, companies are so keen to keep these talented women that they've introduced vital new innovations such as employer-provided daycare.

Even state and local governments have gotten in on the change. In 1928, 61 percent of all school districts would not hire married women, and 52 percent would not retain a woman if she decided to get married.[1] As late as 1967, a married woman in Texas couldn't buy or sell property or even enter into a contract without her husband's permission. In signing a marriage document, a woman was agreeing to sign over virtually every legal decision to her husband, including the right to open a bank account or to make basic decisions for her children. Granted, Texas had one of the worst records in this respect, but many other states had similarly restrictive laws. Today those laws are all gone.[2]

In fairness, we've also seen remarkable changes at the federal level. But considering the degree to which the federal government touches all Americans' lives, and in light of what still remains to be done, it's a disappointing record overall. One major victory was the Civil Rights Act of 1964, outlawing sex discrimination in the workplace. But since then little has been done to update our employees' benefits system to meet the needs of modern, on-the-go families. Similarly, the Social Security system took a leap forward in the 1970s when it became gender neutral. Yet decades later, the program still makes life hard for working couples.

Why are so many of our federal institutions still living in the Dark Ages, even as other organizations have become enlightened? Part of the answer is that many of the organizations that claim to represent women as a whole—groups that wield enormous power in Washington and the media—are actually representing only narrowly defined groups. Their battles over what is best for "women" have helped to keep federal law in limbo.

On the right, groups such as Phyllis Schlafly's Eagle Forum tend to come down on the side of women who have decided to remain in the home, and they support policies that favor women homemakers over women in the labor market. It's not uncommon to see these groups supporting a child tax credit that benefits all parents (whether or not the wife works), but at the same time opposing measures that would lower marginal tax rates for working spouses.

On the left, the National Organization for Women and other feminist groups tend to represent women apart from their roles as spouses and mothers. They push for pay equity and laws against sexual harassment, but have little to say about the economic problems of working mothers and almost nothing to say about discrimination against two-earner couples, such as the marriage tax.

When these two sides meet in combat, often on the rocky terrain of Capitol Hill, it often leads to huge political battles over issues that are fairly trivial. The opposing groups, for instance, spent an enormous amount of time, money, and energy in a fight over the never-adopted Equal Rights Amendment to the Constitution. Yet almost everything supporters of that amendment wanted has already come to pass, without the need for constitutional change. Another bitter struggle was over women in the military, particularly in combat. The fact that very few women actually desire to be in combat was largely ignored.

How do these battles become so fierce when the stakes are so small? It boils down to a conflict of visions, with neither side able see the whole picture. The right tends to idealize the full-time wife and mom. The left tends to idealize the working woman and regard marriage and motherhood as irrelevant. Neither end of the political spectrum has much interest in women who want to be spouse, mother, and wage earner. In a way, these groups are as behind the times as the federal government they seek to influence.

Yet just because a woman has checked into the workforce doesn't mean she's checked out of the rest of her life. Most of the problems we deal with in this book exist precisely because a large and growing number of women seek not only fulfilling careers but to be mothers and wives as well.

Economically, these women who have chosen to do it all are a vibrant and vital part of America's productive engine. They are in every profession, in every job within those professions, and are very good at what they do. It's hard to imagine our economy working without them. Yet this enormous constituency, despite its gains in the business world, has no political representation. They have no political action committees, no advocates to fight for them on national television, no editorial writers trumpeting their cause.

This book seeks to address those issues that have been so ignored by both the right and the left in American politics. Polling and focus groups consistently show that most of the subjects we cover are among women's top concerns. Our goal is to show politicians and voters how the world could be different.

# 2
## ~

# WOMEN AS WORKERS

D AWN FREDETTE, a 46-year-old wife and mother of two living outside of Denver, recently found out what it means to be the full-time breadwinner for her family. It wasn't by choice.

Until a few years ago, Dawn considered her work situation to be "quite fortunate." Her husband Jim worked for the Union Pacific Railroad. It wasn't a job he liked, since it required grueling 80-hour weeks and long periods away from the family. But there was no denying that the big railroad offered fantastic benefits, and so he kept with it. Jim's generous perks also meant that when Dawn's firstborn was a year old and she decided to get part-time work in 1988, the money she earned could go directly toward "making our living a little more enjoyable."

Still, since Jim was on the road and had no control over his hours, Dawn decided she'd only take a job that gave her the freedom to be available for her children. In 1988 she became a paralegal, largely because it allowed her to do part-time contract work. From a flexibility standpoint it was great. She worked two-week contracts here and there and took entire summers off to be with the kids. At one point she stopped work altogether for three years to be with her second child. Along the way she didn't have any employee benefits, but so long as Jim stuck with the railroad they didn't have to worry.

Then things changed. A back injury forced Jim to leave the railroad on disability. His benefits lasted a while, but as they dwindled the Fredettes realized the only economical way to continue health coverage was for Dawn to take a full-time position with a downtown Denver law firm. Today, their life is different.

For starters, Dawn's firm isn't large, and her benefits are small in comparison with what Jim brought home. The company's health plan covers Dawn, but the firm deducts $500 from Dawn's paycheck each month to cover her family—and that doesn't include dental or vision. Her company offers no childcare or education benefits, although she is enrolled in an ongoing retirement plan for the first time in her life.

Things are tight. So tight that to save money Jim has recently considered dropping out of the health plan and claiming VA benefits instead. Dawn worries about the quality of care in the VA program, but notes that in the end, "we may not have a choice."

Notice how many decisions in Dawn and Jim's lives are governed by employee benefits and what people have to do to get them. Millions of Americans have had similar experiences. Yet the employee benefits system is not the product of decisions made in a free labor market. Instead, it has been shaped and molded by government polices.

In fairness, politicians designed these laws with the best of intentions. Laws such as the 1938 Fair Labor Standards Act were created in part to shield hapless laborers from employer abuse, freeing up workers "who toil in factory and on farm to obtain a fair day's pay for a fair day's work."[1] In time, more laws were passed. Employers were allowed to deduct the cost of health insurance provided to employees, even though this opportunity is generally denied to individuals. And regulations barred employers from discriminating against lower-paid workers when they handed out perks. Few politicians could have known along the way that the very changes meant to help employees could ultimately become burdensome obstacles.

The good news is that America has come a long way since the days when Walker Evans produced his searing photographs of Southern sharecroppers, beat down by work and toil. The 21st-century workforce conducts its business via cell phones and laptops, works across world time zones, and makes its office in trains, planes, and cabs. The 1930s laborer went to work so that he could put a loaf of bread on the table. Many couples today tackle two jobs simply because they both want fulfilling careers. Twenty-first-century work issues are no longer about a fair day's pay so much as they are about finding the type of flexible, rewarding job that will allow a worker (and particularly a woman) to juggle career, children, and home life.

The bad news is that work laws have not kept pace with these changing realities. Federal law governs when and how employees may work. It heavily influences what type of benefits they receive. And it even dictates what compensation people qualify for when they are between jobs. Statutes that were once meant to protect workers all too often are rigidly binding the workplace today, preventing arrangements that would be good for both employees and their employers. We live in a country that values freedom and choice above all else, yet we have come to be governed by laws that restrict even the smallest workplace innovation or flexibility.

Dawn and Jim are living examples of how these laws strip away choice. Jim didn't like his railroad job that kept him from his family and might have left it for a more fulfilling one if he hadn't worried about finding similar benefits. Dawn today no longer has the flexibility she wants or needs for her children, since part-time work would leave her family without employer-provided health insurance. What comes next is a description of the major problems people like Dawn and Jim face and how public policies could be updated to reflect modern times.

## PROBLEM NO. 1: THE 40-HOUR STRAITJACKET

Starting all the way back with the Fair Labor Standards Act, the federal government began weighing in on what constituted a full workweek. The ostensible goal was to stop employers from driving workers until they dropped. But there were also other motivations. Union leaders hoped that by encouraging shorter working hours for each employee they would succeed in giving more people a chance to work. The 1930s, after all, was a period of widespread unemployment.

Regardless of the original motivations, little has changed in the past 60 years. The federal government still requires overtime pay for work in excess of 40 hours for large numbers of employees, and in the public psyche the 40-hour-a-week job is still synonymous with "full-time" employment. People who work substantially fewer hours are usually classified as "part-time."

In a modern world in which people work from home, contract out, or carry their duties around with them 24 hours a day via cell phone, the distinction between full-time and part-time work seems very arbitrary. Yet this distinction continues to be *the* defining factor in determining what employees obtain from their place of work in terms of pay and benefits.

Consider a mid-sized legal firm of the sort where Dawn is employed. The firm employs one paralegal in a standard 40-hour week. She's the primary breadwinner in her family, and her husband watches their children. Because she is "full-time," she qualifies for a whole smorgasbord of benefits, including health insurance, paid vacation time, education money, and a retirement plan. If she works past her 40 hours, the law says she must receive overtime pay (time and a half). And she has little or no flexibility in her schedule. She isn't able, say, to save up extra hours she works one week in return for fewer hours the next.

Now consider a second paralegal at the same firm who works a 34-hour week. She is also the primary breadwinner in her family, but since she is a single mother who needs time for her child, she chooses a shorter work schedule. Though she only works a few hours less a week than her 40-hour colleague, she's classified as part-time. This gives her one big advantage over Dawn: a flexible schedule. She can work longer on the days her son has after-school soccer practice so that she gets out earlier on the days he doesn't. But there are also some big disadvantages. She doesn't qualify for health insurance or retirement benefits, for example. She has fewer legal rights should she get in a dispute with her employer. And if she leaves her job, she'll have a much harder time drawing unemployment compensation. In return for flexibility over her work hours, she gives up many, if not all, of the major amenities that come with full-time employment.

There was a time, a Pleasantville time, when the 40-hour system made more sense. Husbands brought home health insurance and other benefits for the whole family and occasionally put in a few long weeks to earn overtime pay for the family vacation. Wives didn't work, and if they did, their time in the workforce was viewed as temporary. In this traditional world, part-time workers didn't need employee benefits since they were likely to be married to a full-time worker who already had them. Granted, this traditional, one-earner, 40-hour world is one that many couples still successfully inhabit. But it is a world that makes no allowances for the growing numbers of people who fall outside the norm, like the 34-hour-a-week paralegal.

The moth-eaten distinctions between full-time and part-time workers particularly bedevil women, since they make up two-thirds of the total part-time workforce.[2] The reason: Women as a whole tend to seek work that fits their lifestyle choices. Many choose fewer hours on the job so that they have more time for home life. Like Dawn in her earlier work years, they market their skills to industries that traditionally or mainly depend on part-time help. Consequently, they find themselves without many of the perks afforded to their full-time peers.

Yet while so much depends on how an employee is categorized, in the end the distinctions are artificial. After all, the 34-hour-a-week paralegal may do the exact same work as her 40-hour colleague and may offer her employer just as much talent. The firm, too, benefits from her schedule if they don't need her more than 34 hours a week. Yet a difference of six hours a week (only six hours!) is all it takes at this company to doom a part-time worker to a world without benefits, legal rights, or other assistance.

In a free labor market, unhindered by worker "protection" legislation, we would expect to find all kinds of innovative working arrangements. The market would accommodate the 40-hour-a-week husband and his stay-at-home wife. But it would also accommodate those husband-wife teams that would each like to work 25- or 30-hour weeks. Employers tend to naturally adjust to worker preferences in competition for labor. If they are allowed to adjust, that is.

The irony is that the 40-hour work week isn't even all that helpful to those couples who still fall into the traditional category of one full-time worker and one stay-at-home spouse. Although some social critics see these arrangements as "pro-family," in reality they encourage the separation of husband, wife, and children.

It works like this: Since neither of two part-time spouses would usually qualify for benefits, one is encouraged to work full-time. Then, if the family needs extra income, it makes more economic sense for the full-timer to stay late at night and work on weekends rather than have the spouse take a part-time job during normal working hours. Why? For starters, the full-timer will get paid time and a half, which is almost certain to be greater than a spouse's part-time wage. Moreover, if the spouse chooses to go to work, she'll get hit with some of the expenses of taking a full-time job—gas for the car or fare for the train or bus, work clothes, and so on—reducing her take-home pay even more.[3] And, as we shall see later, the extra work by the full-timer is likely to add to Social Security benefits later on in life, whereas the part-time spouse's is likely to add nothing.

The upshot is that "traditional" structures encourage one spouse to spend more time away from the family instead of allowing both spouses to carry sensible workloads.

## PROBLEM NO. 2:
## THE INCREDIBLY INFLEXIBLE WORK SCHEDULE

Whatever your view of the traditional one-earner family, the reality is that it is fast becoming a rarity. Women are entering the workforce in greater numbers than ever before and staying at their jobs longer hours. Yet women still take the lead looking after children and home life. The combination of work and family is running straight up against another workplace difficulty: inflexible schedules.

Sixty years ago, just 10 percent of households consisted of dual-earner couples; today, that number is almost 40 percent. Over that same period, the proportion of married couples with just one breadwinner has declined by about one percentage point a year.[4]

Nor does the presence of children seem to change those figures. In 2001, both parents worked in 63 percent of married-couple families with children in school. The numbers are even higher for single mothers: 75 percent with school-aged children were off to work in 2001.[5]

At the same time, jobs have become more demanding and women more ambitious. The result: more hours clocked each week.[6] In 1979, about one-fourth of hourly employees who worked more than 40 hours a week were women; today, it's up to more than one-third. Of those women who put in overtime, almost 40 percent have children under the age of six.

So women sit behind more desks, drive more cranes, and build more computer chips. They do these jobs for longer hours. Yet women also continue to be the primary caregivers for their families. Working mothers are 83 percent more likely to take time off to care for a child than working fathers.[7] And home life, with its soccer practices, doctor's visits, gymnastics lessons, and house repair and maintenance, is more hectic than at any time in the past.

The result is that families in general, and women in particular, are in desperate need of greater flexibility at work. A 1995 poll from the Employment Policy Foundation and Penn and Schoen Associates found that given a choice, three out of every four American workers would choose the option of compensatory time off in lieu of overtime wages (see figure 2.1).[8] The numbers get even higher for women, who struggle harder to juggle work and family life. Some 81 percent of working

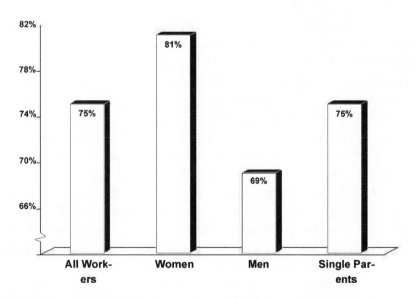

**FIGURE 2.1.** Workers Who Favor Comp Time Option. (Source: Employment Policy Foundation, 1995)

women would choose a job with more flexibility and benefits over a job that offers more pay. And if they have young children, they are feeling escalating pressure. Some 59 percent of mothers with children under six say that it is harder to balance the demands of family and work than it was four years ago.[9]

Public policy, however, is stubbornly rooted in the inflexible past. In general, if full-time employees need time away from the job or want an occasional shorter week, their only option is to dip into vacation time or take leave without pay. On the other hand, if they work beyond 40 hours, labor law requires overtime pay.

The law simply makes very little room for compensatory arrangements, so that longer hours one week can be offset by shorter hours the next. This in turn leads many women to accept positions that they don't enjoy or that pay less, solely to obtain a flexible work schedule.

Ironically, while lawmakers have consistently declined to change these unyielding rules in the private sector, they long ago made work scheduling easier for federal employees. Since 1978, government workers have been free to request alternative work schedules instead of overtime or leave without pay.

And, unsurprisingly, federal workers love the option. Some 46 percent of full-time, hourly federal employees work longer hours in one week and shorter hours the next. The Employment Policy Foundation estimates that if Congress would simply offer the private sector the same freedoms, between 13 million and 20 million Americans would rush to take advantage of such arrangements.[10]

To give credit where it's due, Congress tried. In 1997, then-U.S. Senator John Ashcroft introduced the Family Friendly Workplace Act, specifically citing the need to give women more flexibility over their work schedules. The act would have given companies and their employees three options: a biweekly work schedule that allowed employees to work 80 hours over two weeks in any hourly combination; compensatory time-and-a-half off (an hour and a half off for each overtime hour worked); or flexible credit hours that would allow workers to save up labor past 40 hours one week toward paid leave later on.[11]

The Family Friendly Workplace Act was innovative and very worker friendly. Yet it met fierce opposition from labor unions and (surprisingly!)

even some women's groups. The unions accused Congress of trying to abolish worker protections by getting rid of the 40-hour workweek—a surprising claim given the great success of scheduling flexibility among federal employees. Nonetheless, labor (which theoretically represents workers) marshaled enough support among Senate Democrats to block the bill.

## PROBLEM NO. 3:
## BENEFITS NOT-FOR-ALL

Why did Dawn Fredette choose to move from part-time to full-time work? For one reason and one reason alone: benefits. Of course, Dawn could purchase her benefits outside a job, but she rightly worries it would be "costly." The reason why has to do with a skewed tax system that arbitrarily makes employees dependent on employers for basic goods like health insurance or a retirement plan. Given a choice, many employees might prefer to receive their benefits in cash and then buy their own. But the tax law strongly discourages any such freedom to choose.

On the average, private sector employees receive some 28 percent of their compensation in the form of noncash benefits. This means that out of every $10 the employer "spends" on an employee, the worker receives only $7 in wages.[12] Further, although the $7 of wages is subject to income and payroll taxes, the $3 in benefits escapes all those taxes. From a taxpayer perspective, this is swell for employees. To sweeten the deal, firms are often able to buy health insurance, disability insurance, and life insurance at cheaper prices because of economies of scale.

The downside of all this is that employees are tied to their employers in a lot more ways than they may want to be. Think what would happen if employers stopped paying benefits and paid higher wages instead. An extra $3 in cash wages would quickly morph into only $2 or less after Uncle Sam gets his share. Employees get to dodge the taxman only if the employer pays for the benefits.

Another casualty of this system is fairness. Federal tax subsidies for employee benefits totaled a whopping $306 billion in 2003 and are projected to reach $376 billion by 2009.[13] This is the amount that the federal government *doesn't* collect because employees don't have to pay taxes on benefits. On the average, for every dollar the government collects in personal income taxes, it forgoes another 17 cents because of employee benefits. The cost of this tax loophole equals $1,085 for every man, woman, and child in the country or $2,900 for every American household. Put another way, the average household in America pays almost $3,000 in extra taxes every year so that American workers can have their employee benefits tax free.

But while these tax subsidies are "paid" by all taxpayers, benefits are not enjoyed equally. As demonstrated in figure 2.2, employees of large firms (more than 100 people) are twice as likely to have retirement plans or to receive education benefits as employees of small firms (100 employees or less). Large firms are also twice as likely to provide disability insurance and are more than nine times as likely to offer childcare services.[14]

For better or worse, not everyone lives near a Ford plant or was trained to market products for General Electric. Small firms, for their part, represent the fastest-growing segment of the economy and employ more than half of all workers. But small firms tend to be lean operations:

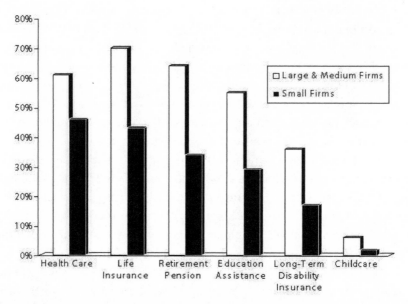

**FIGURE 2.2.** Percent of Employees with Benefits. (Source: "Employee Benefits in Private Industry, 1999," U.S. Bureau of Labor Statistics, News USDL: 01-473, December 19, 2001)

The thousands of pages of rules governing employees' benefits are so confusing and burdensome that many small-business owners throw up their hands in bewilderment. In many cases they lack the money or resources to meet the requirements in the first place.[15] Even if they do put a program in place, they risk running afoul of unsympathetic bureaucrats if they fail to dot every *i* or cross every *t*.

The sad result is that America is evolving into a two-tier system for tax-subsidized employee benefits. On the one hand, some large companies generously provide for every stage of a worker's life: marriage, pregnancy, childcare, divorce, retirement, and even death. Some firms even toss in eldercare, medical coverage for stepchildren, and job search assistance for their employees' spouses. On the other hand, more than a third of small businesses' employees have no health insurance[16] and less than 13 percent have a retirement plan.[17]

Compounding this unfairness, employees who have the best benefits tend to have above-average incomes, while those with few or no perks earn less than average. Many women fall into this latter category. They gravitate toward "pink collar" jobs in retail, trade, and service jobs that are lower paying but easier to pick up and leave when family needs change or they move to another city.[18] The comparisons are stark: Workers in the transportation, public utilities, and durable goods sectors average around $17,629 to $18,000 a year in taxpayer-subsidized benefits, while workers in the service sector receive about half that much and workers in retail trade average just one-fourth (see figure 2.3).

## Problem No. 4: Take-It-or-Leave-It Benefits

Clearly, the worker who receives tax-funded perks is better off than the worker who doesn't—other things being equal. Even so, employer-based benefits aren't a picnic. Federal law may encourage companies to offer perks, but it also runs roughshod over their flexibility.

Strange as it sounds, most benefits are offered on a take-it-or-leave-it basis. Either you take the benefit or you get nothing. As a general rule, employees aren't allowed to forgo their perks and receive higher wages instead.[19] Yet this is wasteful for both companies and employees.

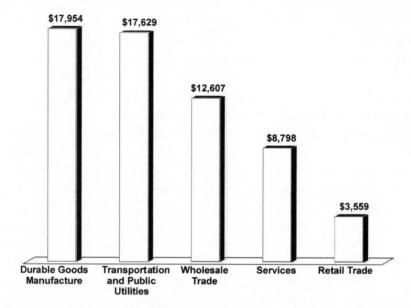

**FIGURE 2.3.** Average Employee Benefits. (Assumes average compensation per industry multiplied by average weekly hours by industry times 52 weeks per year.) (Sources: "Employer Cost for Employee Compensation," U.S. Bureau of Labor Statistics March 2001, Table 16; and Katie Kirkland, "On the Decline in Average Weekly Hours Worked," *Monthly Labor Review*, Vol. 123, No. 7, July 2000, Table I)

Imagine a woman whose husband has generous health insurance coverage for both of them through his job. Since she's already covered, in her job she'd prefer higher wages to a benefit for which she has no use. Her company might also prefer to pay her higher wages, since it could then create a more attractive compensation package and make sure it doesn't lose her valuable skills to some other employer. The only thing standing in the way of this smart economic arrangement is the federal government.[20]

There have been some advances. Some large employers are now allowed to offer "cafeteria" plans, which let employees pick and choose their benefits to some degree. But even cafeteria plans don't solve the problem of two-earner couples. When there are two wage earners, the couple typically only wants one set of benefits plus higher wages rather than duplication.[21]

## PROBLEM NO. 5:
## UNEMPLOYMENT UNASSISTANCE

Like so many other federal work laws, the unemployment system was set up in the 1930s to provide some compensation for down-on-their-luck workers as they searched for new jobs. It's up to the states to administer the program, and rules vary around the nation. Still, the basic idea remains the same: Employers pay taxes on behalf of employees into a fund. Then, if the employees get laid off and are searching for new jobs, they are entitled to draw benefits.

That's the theory. In practice things don't always work so smoothly. Dawn Fredette (through her employer) paid faithfully into the unemployment system all the years she worked in part-time jobs. Yet for all kinds of reasons we'll soon describe, never once did Dawn dip into the Colorado unemployment fund to smooth her transitions in and out of the workforce.

Many people know from hard experience that the design of the unemployment system promotes some bad, unintended consequences. One defect is that the system encourages employers to fire workers in down periods and hire them back when business is good. This encourages workers in seasonal industries to put off finding new jobs.[22] This system also subsidizes unemployment generally by penalizing those who find a job quickly and rewarding those who continue to search.

But a bigger defect for our purposes is that unemployment compensation primarily helps those who lose a full-time job and remain completely unemployed while they search for another full-time job. Part-time employees don't fit this bill. As a result, many pay into the system without ever getting any benefits in return. Dawn is a perfect example.

For starters, unemployment compensation programs are hostile to part-time workers. True, all employees have taxes paid on their behalf, whether they slog through 80-hour weeks or only put in the occasional day. But the rules make it much harder for part-time workers to qualify for benefits if they lose their jobs. The numbers tell the story: Nationwide, only 12 percent of unemployed part-time workers receive unemployment benefits, and full-time workers are almost four times more likely to receive the insurance.[23] The situation is even worse in particular states. In Texas, only 8.5 percent of part-time workers get unemployment, for instance, even though the average Texas part-timer clocks 30 hours a week, 30 weeks a year.[24] Also, the effects are not gender neutral. Nationally, more than twice as many women as men (20 percent versus 8 percent) fail to work the minimum number of weeks required.[25]

The next problem is that unemployment is supposed to be involuntary. There are no allowances for women like Dawn who leave work to have a baby or others who take time off to care for a relative or relocate because of a change in their husband's job. A woman could pay taxes into the system for a decade or more before leaving work to have a child. Not only would she get turned down for benefits during her period out of the workforce, in most states she'd also be denied help when she reenters the labor force and searches for a new job.[26]

To add insult to injury, if she does find a job, works for a month and *then* is laid off, she *still* won't qualify for benefits. That's because all but nine states ignore the most recent three to six months of work when calculating eligibility for unemployment compensation.[27]

It doesn't have to be this way. Why not allow all workers to pay into unemployment accounts they own? In periods of nonwork (whatever the reason may be), people could draw from their accounts to pay their rent, search for a job, or acquire new education or training. A "privatized" system would let people move freely in and out of the labor market and wouldn't penalize such activities as having a child.[28]

The good news is that we know a system like this can work. Chile recently implemented a system of individual unemployment accounts, and the results have had officials buzzing the world over. Chilean workers and their employers pay a small percentage of their wages into an individual account, while employers make a separate contribution into a pooled account. Workers can draw from their individual funds whenever they are unemployed, for whatever reason, and should they exhaust this money they can also draw from the general pool. Also, workers eventually get to keep any of their own account money they don't spend.

Consider the advantages: The funds in individual accounts become available to Chilean laborers whether they quit, are fired, or retire. Workers have a real incentive to minimize their unemployment time, since they use up money they would otherwise have for retirement. And the Chilean system gets rid of the need for adjudication (to determine the legitimacy of claims), which is a costly process in the United States.[29]

## WHAT CAN BE DONE?

Dawn Fredette, like millions of American women, is a committed employee, with the training and experience to make her a prized addition to companies and the workforce. She is also, like millions of American women, a committed mother and wife who believes in nurturing her children, supporting her husband, and keeping together a happy home. Yet again and again, women like Dawn run up against a system that seems determined to make it impossible for them to do both.

These women confront labor regulations written with full-time workers in mind. Anyone who can't meet that arbitrary distinction— active moms and dads, caregivers for elderly parents, and so on—is locked out of the world of benefits, legal rights, and social insurance benefits. Even couples that fall into the traditional one-earner category suffer under the system, because it encourages one spouse to log long work hours to the detriment of family life rather than dividing a shorter workweek between the two spouses.

That system has created two classes of Americans: full-time employees who receive benefits (often at large firms), and those who are left searching. Even those families that do secure benefits through their employers have no recourse should both spouses' benefits duplicate one another.

Women are especially hurt by an unemployment compensation system that is geared toward full-time workers who become unemployed and then return to yet another full-time job. Women who move in and out of the workforce for children or other commitments find that the unemployment taxes their employers dutifully paid for them during their years of employment produce few, if any, benefits.

Many employers and employees long ago realized that the modern world demands a system with far more flexibility and choice and have been asking Congress for relief. The only question is whether reactionary forces will continue to hold labor law prisoner in the regulatory dark ages. If and when reform of tax law, labor law, and employee benefits law happens, it should:

- give companies the freedom to offer employees choices between benefits and higher wages[30];
- give companies and their employees the freedom to set up flexible work schedules—so that workers can balance the tough tradeoff between work and family life;
- allow workers who have to obtain health insurance and other benefits on their own a tax break similar to the tax subsidy given to on-the-job benefits; and
- convert the unemployment insurance system into a system of private accounts, so that it no longer penalizes part-time workers or those who move in and out of the labor market because of family obligations.

These reforms are not merely good things to do. They are essential steps in making federal law consistent with the realities of family life in the 21st century.

# 3
~

# WOMEN AND CHILDCARE

AMY,[1] A MIDDLE school band teacher in the Dallas area, was still pregnant with her first daughter when she started her hunt for childcare. She knew that her small school district didn't offer childcare help and that it would be up to her and her husband to go through the complicated process of finding someone to watch their baby—someone they could trust, who was affordable, and who would fit in with their work schedules.

Amy's first discovery was that the school where she worked was in a wealthy neighborhood and daycare cost much more than where she lived. Some of the daycare facilities ran up to $300 a week and required schoolteachers like Amy to pay up to $75 a week during the summer months when she didn't need help just to "hold" a space for when the child returned in the fall. These high prices remind Amy of a fellow teacher who currently pays so much for childcare that she takes home only $250 of her paycheck each month. This friend has been thinking of leaving her job.

But Amy didn't want to quit; she loves her position and says she couldn't imagine not having the interaction with the kids in her band classes or the fulfillment that comes with her work. As it happened, it was a colleague who ended up referring her to a local woman who looks after fellow teachers' children.

Amy couldn't have asked for more. The daycare provider is only five minutes from her school and flexible about drop-off and pick-up times. Amy was thrilled to find through her visits that the woman, who has three children of her own, was "completely wonderful with kids." Amy's 14-month-old daughter looks forward each day to attending, and Amy is comforted to know that her daughter spends her days with children of colleagues and other parents Amy knows and likes. Best of all, this service and peace of mind came with a reasonable price tag of $110 a week.

The downside of the current situation is that Amy's daycare is "informal." So far as Amy knows, the woman does not have an official license to run a daycare facility and is paid in cash, which means that if Amy and her husband try to claim a tax credit, they can't supply the proper documentation if they are audited by the IRS. They talked briefly about alternatives but in the end decided that any tax credit they received would be wiped out by the higher prices they'd pay to send their daughter to a licensed facility. A tax credit would be nice, says Amy, but right now "it's up to us."

The childcare hurdles that Amy and other mothers must jump are a new and daunting challenge for modern families. In the 1930s, when some of our most important laws and institutions first evolved, very few women with children were in the workplace. The policy makers of the time never even considered a world in which both parents would go off to offices or work sites, much less one in which growing numbers of single parents are left wondering how to juggle home and family life.

But that's today's world, and one in which it is becoming harder for working families to find workable solutions for their work and childcare needs. Over the past 60-some years, the number of working women with children under the age of six has grown at a rate of about one percentage point a year. Today, more than 60 percent of women with children under age six are in the labor market (see figure 3.1).[2]

These working families run a gauntlet of public policies that combine to discourage mothers from holding productive jobs. The tax code still rewards moms who stay at home and punishes those who enter the workforce. Women who work for wages find that there is rarely adequate tax relief for childcare expenses. In many cases the relief that exists is arbitrary, flowing to those families fortunate enough to work for a big

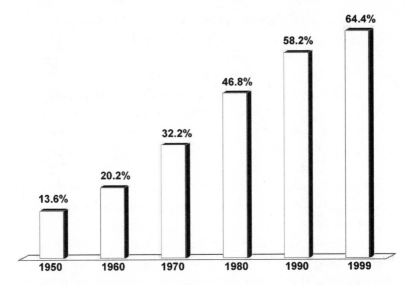

**FIGURE 3.1.** Percent of Mothers with Children under Age 6 in Paid Workforce. (Source: "Table 9-1, Labor Force Participation Rates of Women, by Presence and Age of Youngest Child, Selected years 1947–99," U.S. Department of Labor, Bureau of Labor Statistics)

company and drying up for those who work for a small business, or for women like Amy who depend on informal childcare. Some families find it impossible to even procure adequate daycare services, given a maze of laws and regulations that bar new providers and drive up daycare costs. What follows is a breakdown of these many hurdles and some suggestions for improving the situation.

## PROBLEM NO. 1:
## THE NOT-SO-HAPPY HOMEMAKER

Imagine for a moment that the federal government passed a law requiring that all families with children have at least one parent who stays at home with the kids full-time. Americans would be rightly incensed if Congress got in the business of telling ordinary citizens whether to work or not.

Yet the federal government is very much in that business; it just happens to exercise its influence through the tax code rather than through decree. The first big difficulty women face when it comes to childcare is that the government rewards mothers who do it themselves and makes life difficult for those who choose to hire others to do it for them. Our current tax law favors productive activities in the home but deals harshly with those exact same activities if they take place in the marketplace.

Imagine a fictional Wilma, a mother who has long played the role of the stay-at-home spouse. She has spent many days cooking lunches and dinners, doing the laundry, mowing the lawn, and reading stories at nap-time. Wilma is working just as much as the paralegal in our last chapter who spends her days in an office. Yet the "income" this stay-at-home mom produces is known as "imputed income" (because no actual money changes hands). Economists estimate that imputed income nationwide is as much as one-third of national income.[3] But the Internal Revenue steers clear, choosing to tax only income that is earned in the marketplace.

Now imagine that Wilma gets a yen to restart her career. She leaves her home to take a job in marketing and employs Betty, a neighbor, to perform all those tasks that she had previously done in her home.

It is at this point that Wilma, our marketing executive, discovers the first unfairness of today's system: She is taxed fully on her wages, but is not allowed any deductions for her out-of-pocket payments to Betty. Wilma soon finds that the combination of the taxes she pays on her own wages and the money she pays to Betty for childcare and housework means that she only keeps about one-third of what she earns.

Betty, meanwhile, discovers the second unfairness of the system: She has to pay taxes for doing the same childcare and cleaning that Wilma had previously done untaxed. Assuming that Betty pays a self-employment payroll tax of 15.3 percent and an income tax rate of 15 percent, she'll have watched children and made lunches and washed clothes all day to take home 70 cents out of every dollar she earned. If her husband works, she'll be thrown into an even higher tax bracket and may keep only half her earnings.

In these ways, federal tax policy subsidizes women who work in the home and taxes women who work for wages—even if these women are performing the same jobs. Wilma and Betty did the exact work—childcare, cooking, cleaning, yard work—and for the same number of hours. Wilma was not taxed to do this work but Betty was. It would be little wonder if Wilma were convinced by the tax and expense realities to give up her career and stay at home again with her children. Likewise it would be no surprise if Betty decided it wasn't worthwhile to provide valuable outside services to others given her take-home pay. In the end, the tax code strongly encourages both women to quit their jobs (much in the way it has encouraged Amy's friend to quit hers) whether they want to or not.

The point of this book isn't to make any judgments as to whether moms and dads should stay at home or go to work. That is fundamentally a personal decision that only parents can make. But if moms and dads both decide to go to work, they are faced with a baffling array of policies that impact their childcare decisions. They want to choose the kind of care that best fits their situation and is best for their children but find that federal policies encourage commercial centers and not others. They may have access to a commercial, quality childcare center but simply don't want to enroll their children there.[4]

Parents may be unsure about effects of commercial childcare on children and choose to employ a trusted neighbor instead. As for evidence on the effects of commercial childcare, there's grist for all sides of the debate.[5] In the future, there will be more studies and more debates. But that's not a reason for the government to be involved in parents' decisions. A much better approach would be a level playing field—where the government neither encourages nor discourages family choices through tax policy.

There are ways to do this, though most of them would admittedly take some dramatic new thinking from lawmakers. One way of going about it would be to create a broad taxpayer deduction for people like Wilma, who purchase homemaker services from others. On the opposite end of the spectrum, we could exempt from taxation people like Betty, who provide such homemaker services for pay.

There is, however, an easier first step toward greater neutrality, one that doesn't involve creating entire new sections of the tax code. It involves providing more families with access to tax breaks that already exist for those lucky enough to take advantage of them.

## PROBLEM NO. 2:
## SCRATCHING FOR TAX DOLLARS

Despite the fact that childcare wasn't considered in early social policy, the idea of giving families some sort of relief for their childcare expenses came about pretty quickly and has been around for 50 years. In the very early days, childcare was treated as a "business expense" and families up to a certain income level were allowed to take a deduction. Slowly, that tax deduction morphed into a combination of exemptions, tax credits, and other subsidies, which is the complex system we have today.[6]

Regardless of income and employment, all parents are eligible for the dependency exemption. Families with dependent children are allowed to deduct a set amount from their taxes for each child. For 2003, the dependency exemption was $3,050. Next, there is the Child Tax Credit. Tax law allows a tax credit to all low- to high-middle-income families. This tax credit makes no distinction between working and stay-at-home parents. For 2003 and 2004, the credit was $1,000 for each qualifying child.[7]

Finally, working parents are eligible for the Child and Dependent Care Tax Credit (CDCTC). The amount of tax relief families actually receive depends partly on their income and partly on their expenses. Parents who are full-time wage earners can claim from 20 to 35 percent of qualified childcare expenses for children under age 13 against their income tax liability.[8] If there are two married parents in the household, both must work to be eligible. The credit percentage goes down the more parents earn, and the expenses that can be claimed are capped. For 2004, parents could claim expenses up to $3,000 for one child and $6,000 for two or more children. Thus, a mother who pays $3,000 or more for childcare and earns $15,000 or less would be able to deduct $1,050 (35 percent × $3,000) from her taxes. However, if her income was $43,000 or more, she can deduct only $600 (20 percent × $3,000) from her tax liability. She can reduce her taxes by twice those amounts if she has two or more children.

But actual childcare expenses tend to average about $286 a month per child, and can be a whole lot more.[9] If Amy had chosen to use a $300-a-week commercial daycare facility, her costs for even 10 months a year of work would have come to around $12,000—and she'd have only been able to claim a fraction of that. All of which illustrates that the current Dependent Care Tax Credit is way too small relative to actual costs.

That being said, there's a lot of evidence to suggest that even the somewhat small DCTC that exists today has gone a long way toward injecting a little neutrality into the tax code, allowing greater numbers of women to follow their careers if they so choose. No one knows for certain just how many mothers choose to work because of the DCTC, but the evidence suggests quite a few.[10] One of the best examples that tax credits are grabbed up are the results of the Tax Reform Act of 1981, which created a far more generous childcare tax credit as well as other tax incentives for working mothers. Following these reforms, the number of families who claimed the tax credit on their IRS forms soared— from five million in 1982 to nine million in 1986. But when the Family Support Act of 1988 required more paperwork to claim the credit, the number dropped back to six million in 1989, and the credit never regained its former popularity.

Of course, even the Child Tax Credit (the flat credit given to taxpayers whether or not they are working) isn't without its critics. The biggest complaint is that it amounts to a federal subsidy to the middle class and wealthy. And it's true that less than 10 percent of Child Tax Credit dollars go to families that earn under $20,000, while more than 67 percent of returns are made to families with incomes between $20,000 and $75,000. In fact, during the 1990s, the percentage of the credit going to families making more than $75, 000 increased from 10 to 25 percent![11] But the disparity isn't the result of tax authorities having something against low-income families. Rather, it's because most low-income families don't pay income tax in the first place. The tax credit isn't refundable and so can't be claimed by those who owe no money to the government.

Also, there are the economic benefits to tax relief for childcare. Women who choose to work because they have their children cared for make a contribution to the economy, adding to the nation's output of goods and services. The wages these women earn generate new tax revenues—federal income and payroll taxes, state and city income taxes, and employment taxes. And all the new tax revenue Uncle Sam collects from women's wages helps pay for the tax credit the good man handed out in the first place.

Of course, the goal of tax policy isn't just to allow the federal government to rake in money. But what childcare tax credits do show is that not all tax cuts and federal spending are created equal. If the choice is between giving a woman a welfare check because she can't afford the childcare expenses that come with a job or giving her a generous childcare tax credit that allows her to contribute to the economy and generate new tax revenues, the tax credit is clearly a far more productive use of government money.

## Problem No. 3:
## Tax Relief for You . . . But Not for You[12]

Given the size of our tax code, it should come as no surprise to find that the credits allowed to individual taxpayers aren't the only way the federal government subsidizes childcare. Congress also allows employers to set up Dependent Care Spending Accounts, giving employees the opportunity to set aside as much as $5,000 a year of pretax wages to help purchase childcare services.[13] A family that falls into a 50 percent tax bracket, for instance, gets a subsidy of $2,500 a year in reduced taxes.

But perhaps the biggest subsidy of all goes to larger companies that provide daycare facilities for their employees. These companies cannot only deduct all the costs but can also qualify for special tax credits under federal and state income tax laws.[14] Plus, this is yet another employee benefit that escapes the income and payroll taxes employees ordinarily pay. But as we mentioned in the previous chapter, only the biggest companies typically offer such benefits. Millions of small businesses around the country would like to give their employees a helping hand but can't manage the base costs of getting a daycare facility running or are overwhelmed by the tangle of bureaucratic red tape that comes with complying with all the laws. In establishments with more than 5,000 workers, an impressive 45.8 percent of employees have access to childcare services; but in companies with fewer than 100 workers that number drops to a tiny 4.5 percent.[15]

What this means is that the government is subsidizing extraordinary corporate childcare tax benefits—benefits that may far outpace the DCTC or a spending account—to only a small slice of the labor pool.

## PROBLEM NO. 4:
## NO RECEIPT, NO HELP

While the government is providing generous help to mothers who work for big companies, it is neglecting a far larger number who depend on informal services for their childcare help. An Urban Institute study finds that an amazing 60 percent of low-income families do not officially pay for childcare, either because the care is provided free of charge or because costs are paid by the government, another organization, or another individual. Relatives or others within a child's home care for 74 percent of children under the age of five in households at or below 200 percent of the federal poverty line.[16]

Yet because these services are not purchased in the marketplace, parents have no receipts for their out-of-pocket expenses. Those expenses might include paying a provider under the table. But even families who rely on "free" daycare from relatives still face expenses, whether it be gas money or bus fare to transport their child to a relative's house, providing that relative with an insured vehicle to take the child to doctor's appointments or play dates, or giving the relative money for lunches or dinners. These might seem like incidental expenses, but over the course of a year they can add up to a significant chunk of money.

There is also a related problem: even when there are out-of-pocket expenses, only certain kinds of outlays count. For instance, in order to count payments to a friend or relative, the caregiver has to be treated as an employee, with income and payroll taxes deducted and sent to Uncle Sam. If the child is in a facility outside the home, that facility has to comply with all the cost-increasing regulations that apply to commercial daycare.[17]

The way in which we subsidize childcare, therefore, ignores how most childcare services are provided. It does not have to be that way. Tax relief for raising children should be available to parents who make informal arrangements for childcare. The general practice of providing the most tax relief for childcare expenses when payments are made to licensed centers is tantamount to providing a tax subsidy to the centers. This situation has led to the growth of a special interest group, a lobbying coalition that includes the daycare industry and its champions. Tax code support for commercial, accredited centers is unfair to parents who prefer other forms of childcare and subsidizes an industry that is unwanted by the majority of parents.

Needless to say, a lot of parents fall through all these cracks in the tax code. Overall, only 28 percent of working parents take their children to commercial childcare centers. Most parents use care provided by relatives or in family childcare homes.[18]

Take the case of Lori Garofalo, a legal secretary who works for a midsize law firm in Denver. Lori feels fortunate that her mother-in-law has been around to watch her three children over the years she's worked, especially because neither her law firm nor her husband's private school (where he is a teacher) offered help. Lori also points out that their financial situation is such that they both need to work to cover bills and extras, and would have been hard pressed to both stay in their jobs if faced with formal daycare expenses.

Even so, the Garofalos did pay for the childcare. Lori said she "didn't feel right" not giving her mother-in-law something for all the work she did. Between the small stipend she paid, as well as extra money for food and diapers and other incidentals, Lori estimates that they put out anywhere from $400 to $500 a month for childcare—and that was with a relative who was officially watching their children for "free." Yet because this was informal care, they were unable to claim a federal tax credit. And Lori points out that even if they had been able to claim federal help, the complicated formula used to calculate the credit meant they would have gotten very little money back.

Fixing this system wouldn't take much. If both parents are working full-time, the government should be able to reasonably assume that the family is incurring real childcare costs. Similarly, the government should be able to assume that a single mother or father working full-time is racking up real childcare expenses. Tax authorities should have a provision whereby parents who fall into these categories can claim some sort of tax relief without all the formalities of an official bill of goods. And that tax relief should also be generous enough to make claiming it worth the parents' efforts.

## PROBLEM NO. 5:
## DYING FOR DAYCARE

A family's struggle to scrape up the money for childcare is only half the battle. Assuming parents can make it work financially, they then get the unsavory task of trying to find an individual whom they trust to leave their children with for long periods of the day. Unfortunately, many pockets of the country still face real shortages of childcare services.

This is a strange thing since the market appears able to readily expand. Childcare researcher Alison Hagy says that over the past 20 years the demand for paid childcare has doubled, but the real (inflation adjusted) price of that care has not really changed. This suggests that, in the country as a whole, enough childcare facilities have opened up to keep pace with demand.[19]

In those places where shortages exist the culprit is often overly strict (if not downright silly) regulations. Take the real-life story of a Berkeley, California, company that wanted to set up a daycare facility for its employees.[20] It was a nice idea; employees at the firm would be able to drop off and pick up their kids from the same place they worked and would even be on hand for an occasional lunch or tears. A nice idea, that is, until the company started to investigate the insane laws with which it would have to comply.

The company was told that to get a license, it would have to ensure that its daycare facility didn't share any common ground with the rest of the building. It would need a separate entrance, separate bathrooms, and a separate kitchen. But that wasn't all. It was also told that California's licensing law required 35 square feet per child inside the building and 75 square feet outside.

Even assuming the firm was willing or financially able to comply with such craziness, an entire other set of laws made it impossible. As it happened, Berkeley's local zoning ordinances forbade the company to make a separate entrance, bathroom, and kitchen. And the space requirements were wishful thinking in an urban city setting. The company packed in its plans for a daycare facility, and parents went looking for other options.

In theory, home-based daycare in particular would be a magical solution to many of the nation's daycare needs. It would help solve daycare shortages in parts of the country and would be ideal for the many women entrepreneurs who have proven themselves so adept at running home-based companies.

Today, anywhere from 10 to 12 million businesses are run from home. Half of all women-owned businesses are run out of living rooms and dens,[21] and the number of businesses owned by women is growing at twice the rate of businesses overall.[22] With track records like these and with so many women who prefer work that allows them to stay at home with their own children, it should be natural for more mothers to get in the business of quality daycare services. Instead, they find themselves facing the same sort of regulation as our company in Berkeley.

No less than 90 percent of all U.S. cities today place restrictions on home-based work. Reasonable people may disagree over the need for local governments to impose minimum workplace standards on homes, but the majority of the regulations on the books defy common sense. They include requirements that no outside employees may work in a home; that only one family member may work in the business; and that only one room of a house may be used for business purposes. Other rules require that a separate entrance is maintained for business customers, or that no business inventory may be stored in a garage.[23] And childcare licensing is even more complex. Some of the state licensure manuals for childcare facilities are so complex (running to hundreds of pages) that a fully-qualified attorney would have difficulty deciphering the language, much less an ordinary mom who wanted to watch a few children in her home each day.

Surely, you think, officials don't really enforce these requirements down to the letter? Think again. Local officials told one California woman that in order to have a childcare facility in her home she had to supply separate bathrooms for teachers and for children, to install commercial (rather than household) locks on her doors, and install a commercial thermostat on her refrigerator. In case that wasn't a big enough hassle, she also had to get the approval of 14 of her neighbors in nearby homes and ensure that no child arrive before 8:00 in the morning or remain past 5:30 in the afternoon.[24]

These licensing laws, zoning regulations, and antihome-work statutes don't just have the effect of putting a crimp on the market for daycare.

They also take valuable choices away from parents. Thousands of working mothers like Amy would prefer to leave their child with a trusted community member, in a home full of children of neighbors and friends. But regulations often impose arbitrary and impossible-to-meet restrictions on average providers. The result is that many parents instead have to take their children to licensed daycare facilities that are expensive and unfamiliar—and might not be what's best for their child.

The unfortunate thing is that it is often these very licensed facilities that are behind home-based regulations, since they have a financial interest in maintaining their monopoly over care.[25] They spend significant time and money lobbying government to keep the most onerous restrictions in place. Many also play on public fears that without such strict regulation, children will be subject to abuse—particularly sexual abuse. This fear campaign has been effective, even if the reality is that child-sex scandals are few and far between.

What the regulation proponents rarely mention is that even a thousand laws will do little to inform families about the type of care their children will really receive from any given daycare provider, and often the laws can backfire.[26] Regulations, for instance, did nothing to stop a Colorado daycare operator who was previously acquitted of sexual abuse charges on grounds of insanity from taking in more kids. Yet the very same set of laws might prevent a mature and well-qualified woman from looking after children because she was unlucky enough to get caught smoking marijuana when she was 15 years old.

In the end, government agencies have only one real advantage over parents: agencies are more easily able to gather basic data about childcare providers such as credentials, training, or service records. But much of the information that families really need—for instance, a sense of how good the provider is with children—can only be obtained by parents who make frequent visits and onsite inspections. Regulatory agencies, often located in a distant city or understaffed, simply aren't equipped to tell mom or dad whether little Susie will be happy or safe with any one provider.

By putting together a dossier of basic information, agencies may well be able to help parents make better-informed choices. But once that information is shared, it should be parents—not officials measuring square footage or checking for commercial thermometers—who make the judgment as to whether a daycare provider is qualified to look after their little ones.[27]

## What Can Be Done?

Taken as a whole, the only uniting theme behind this hodgepodge of childcare help is that it has largely been an afterthought. Basic federal policy is still premised on the notion that childcare expenses will be rare and unusual rather than an ongoing and integral part of family life that play a huge role in the economy. Over time, officials have tacked on provisions here and there, all meant to give some sort of relief. But a look at the Child Tax Credit alone—which until recently hadn't changed in close to two decades—shows that Congress has yet to give any real or sustained attention to the radical changes in family life that occurred in the past half century.

Rather than dabbling, Congress should be encouraged to take a sweeping new approach to childcare policies. Any reform should

- encourage flexibility in labor law and employee benefits law so that parents who prefer to take care of their own children have a greater opportunity to do so;
- allow working parents who use informal childcare services to claim the credit;
- make the Dependent Care Spending Account universal: working parents who don't claim the Dependent Care Tax Credit should be able to deduct up to $5,000 in expenses;
- free potential daycare providers from onerous state and local laws that are largely molded by special interest groups and serve primarily to prevent parents from obtaining high-quality childcare; and
- recognize that while government agencies may have an integral role in gathering and communicating information about daycare providers, they should play little other role in regulating childcare services; parents are usually better placed to make pertinent decisions about the people who watch their children.

4
~

# WOMEN AS TAXPAYERS

NOT LONG AFTER Mary finished high school, she entered the nursing field. For close to seven years she made a good living and enjoyed her job, earning nearly $20 an hour as a surgical assistant in Las Vegas.

Around 1996, she met and married Lee, and they moved for his job to North Carolina. The pay for Mary's type of work wasn't nearly as good in that area, and she wanted to spend more time at home with her son. So she quit. Since then, Mary and Lee have moved to a rural town in Oregon and now have three children.

As her children have grown, Mary has often thought of going back to the work that she enjoyed. But every time she considers it, economics get in the way. For starters, the average pay for a surgical assistant or equivalent job as a medical assistant in her part of Oregon is about $7 to $10 an hour, or $14,000 to $20,000 a year. Since Lee earns $65,000 a year, Mary's salary would be added to that for tax purposes—which means she'd automatically face a 25 percent federal income tax rate (if she were single, she'd pay only 15 percent). She'd also face a state income tax and Social Security taxes, which could push her tax burden close to more than 40 percent.

After the taxes were taken out, Mary would also have to pay for daycare for her three children—full-time care for her youngest and after-school or summer holiday care for the two oldest. Mary figures that this would run $150 to $200 a week or as much as $10,000 a year. After adding up the taxes and outside expenses, she discovered that there was a good chance that she'd end up "losing" money by going to work. "Even in a best case financial scenario, I just can't justify it," she says.

It's fair to say that taxes have been at the root of more heated political discussion in America than perhaps any other issue in the history of the country, from the Boston Tea Party to Shays' Rebellion. Even today, an issue in just about every federal election is whether candidates are likely to raise or lower the amount the federal government takes from our paychecks.

Polls continue to show that the majority of Americans feel they are overtaxed. Some want across-the-board relief and others want targeted cuts. A minority believes that the general public should pay more than they already do so that the government can provide more services. There are also questions about wealth and fairness, such as whether the "rich" should pay a greater percentage of their income to the taxman than the "poor."

What many of these debates about fairness ignore, however, is that a large number of Americans who do not think of themselves as "wealthy" already pay a disproportionate amount to the federal government. Who are these luckless folk? Married couples.

Our income tax system evolved at a time when very few families had both a husband and a wife in the labor market. That's changed to the point that some two-thirds of married women today are on the job (see figure 4.1). Yet, the system is hugely biased against two-earner couples. All too often, the lower-earning spouse, who more often than not is a woman, hands over a much bigger chunk of her paycheck to the government than she would if she were single.

And that isn't all. Women who go to work face extra expenses, such as childcare and paid housekeeping, which combine to eat up a big portion of their after-tax wages and make it that much harder to justify a career. Even low-income earners face harsh penalties when their marginal tax rates are combined with the withdrawal of government aid. And the lifetime consequences of working, in terms of taxes and a loss of benefits, can make even the most ambitious women wonder if a two-earner household is such a great idea. Following are a few of the difficulties, presented in greater depth.

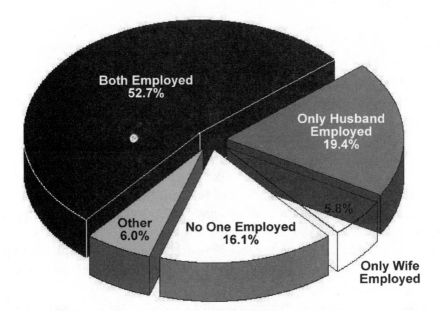

**FIGURE 4.1.** Employment Characteristics of Married Couple Families (2001). (Source: Bureau of Labor Statistics, "Employment Characteristics of Families Summary," Table 2, March 29, 2002)

## PROBLEM NO. 1:
## FOR RICHER, OR MUCH POORER

As anyone who has done it will attest, the decision to get married isn't simple. There are those nagging little things: Can you live with a spouse who leaves wet bath towels on the floor or who loses the house keys? There are the difficult in-laws to consider and whether you are ready for children who will leave toy trains on the stairs. Added to that is the question of whether you're willing to pay a whole lot more in taxes for the privilege of saying "I do."

The question of how to tax married couples has been around for a long time, with the government seemingly unable to make up its mind as to whether tying the knot should be rewarded or penalized.[1] When the income tax first arrived in 1913, there was no distinction between married and unmarried taxpayers. Then, starting in the 1920s, couples living in states with community property laws were allowed to assign half their income to each spouse for tax purposes, even if all the earnings were produced by only one person. This practice often put the couple in a lower tax bracket and lowered their tax burden significantly. By 1948, every couple in America was allowed to divide their joint income when calculating their taxes.

The ability of married couples to split their taxable income created for many a "marriage bonus." In fact, by 1969 a bachelor could conceivably pay 40 percent more in taxes than the married couple next door earning the same income. In response to complaints, that year Congress created a difference between married and single filers. Unfortunately, the reform went so far in the other direction that it created a "marriage penalty." Suddenly it became a real financial downer for many people to be married. As salaries have increased in the country, the marriage penalty has hit more and more couples.

The reason for the problem is our progressive tax code, in which higher incomes are socked by higher tax rates. Simply put, when a second earner in any household (like Mary in our previous example) adds her income to the primary earner's, she is often pushed into a higher tax bracket.

Let's imagine Alice, a stay-at-home wife who is married to Ralph, a bus driver earning $25,000 year. Ralph and Alice have enough deductions and exemptions so that they fall into the 10 percent income tax bracket. In addition, Ralph's share of the FICA payroll tax (7.65 percent) takes a total of 18 cents out of each extra dollar he earns. Now assume that Alice begins working as a distributor for Mary Kay Cosmetics. Initially she doesn't earn much, but it's enough to push the couple into the 15 percent tax bracket. In time, Alice becomes more successful. She persuades a number of her friends to work for Mary Kay, and she gets a commission on all of their sales. When her income reaches $50,000 the couple is pushed into the 25 percent federal tax bracket and faces a 7.5 percent state and local income tax as well. This means that Ralph is now losing 40 cents out of each additional dollar he earns, including overtime pay.

Finally, Alice hits the jackpot, and her income soars to $300,000. At this point, the couple is in the 35 percent tax bracket, and when Social Security and state and local taxes are figured in, Ralph finds that half of his income is going to taxes, even though his salary has not changed by a penny.[2]

In short, Ralph gets slapped with higher and higher taxes solely because of Alice's earnings. He hasn't changed jobs. He isn't earning more. In fact, nothing about his life is different from any time in the past. Yet Ralph now pays the government 35 cents more out of each dollar of salary then he did before. Eventually, Ralph may wonder if it is worthwhile to continue working. Ralph and Alice might even begin to question whether it makes financial sense for them to stay married. Such are the perversities of tax law.

Now consider a more common situation. Imagine Ed, who runs his own sewage-treatment company and brings home about $85,000 a year. His wife, Trixie, is pretty good in the kitchen and decides to go to work for a catering firm. Trixie's first paycheck holds some nasty surprises.

Trixie's first job pays only the minimum wage, but since her salary is added to Ed's $85,000 she automatically pays 25 cents of each dollar she earns to the federal government. When she looks at the next column of the pay stub, she finds that state and local taxes have made her rate closer to 33 percent.

And it gets worse. While the income tax laws treat couples as a single unit, the Social Security (FICA) tax acts as though they don't know each other. Ed may have already paid the maximum in Social Security taxes, but Trixie must also begin paying the tax on her very first dollar of wages. So Trixie discovers that the federal government has taken yet another 7.65 percent of her salary away to pay for Social Security (the other half is paid by her employer), bringing her total tax rate to 41 percent—the penalty for earning a minimum wage income.

It could be worse. If Trixie starts her own catering business, as a self-employed woman she will pay both portions of the FICA tax. Even though she may still be earning the equivalent of the minimum wage, Trixie would be handing over close to half of her income in taxes (see figure 4.2). Trixie, like Ralph in the previous example, may well decide that the work isn't worth it, and pack in what might otherwise be a productive business.

In recent years, we've heard a lot about the "marriage penalty" that so burdens the Ralphs and Trixies of the world along with their spouses.

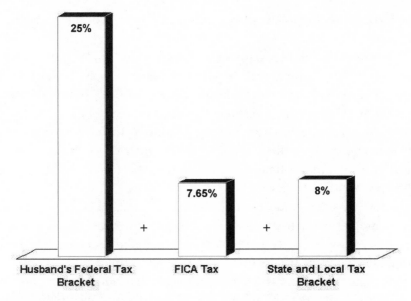

**FIGURE 4.2.** Components of the Marginal Tax Rate (for a woman married to a middle-income husband)

President George W. Bush has condemned it, as have any number of Republicans and Democrats in Congress. One of the objectives of both the 2001 and 2003 tax cuts was to reduce it, and both pieces of legislation purported to do just that.

But the marriage penalty is only part of the problem. The other issue is the very high marginal tax rates faced by the spouse in a two-earner couple. In dealing with the first issue, Congress did very little about the second. The 2001 and 2003 tax relief measures were pro-marriage for many middle-income couples. They now have less financial reason to divorce. But we are still hitting second earner spouses with draconian tax rates.

## Problem No. 2:
## All the Extras

Trixie and Ed know what it means to be penalized with higher taxes for having taken their vows. But paying more than half your salary to the government is only one of the financial expenses that come with going to work. No couple can escape an increase in out-of-pocket expenses.

In most cases, a stay-at-home spouse is providing all kinds of services to the family. These services include going shopping and making meals, keeping the house clean, doing the yard work, and watching the children. In most cases, if that stay-at-home spouse decides to go to work, a lot of these services will now have to be purchased from others.

In theory it is possible for a family to still do everything themselves, but that's rarely what happens in reality. When spouses both work, free time becomes more precious. After a long day's work, they are reluctant to get back into the car, drive to the supermarket, and spend another hour preparing dinner. So they order some take-in food instead. It's tempting to send the work shirts out for laundering rather than spend an hour over an ironing board. After trying to keep up with mopping and vacuuming on evenings and Saturdays, they give in and hire a part-time housekeeper. And as we know from the stories of Amy and Lori Garafolo in the last chapter, there is simply no way of avoiding reliance on others for trusted childcare.

Consider again the case of Mary in Oregon. For most women who decide to go to work, it is reasonable to assume that they will spend at least one-fourth of their earnings on replacement services.[3] In Mary's case, even the best-case scenario found her paying close to one-third of her total salary in childcare alone, and that was before taking into account any other expense, like paid housekeeping. Once you add up her taxes and childcare, Mary, like many women, faces an "effective" tax rate of at least 65 percent on her income. Put another way, for every dollar that Mary earns in her job, at most she and Lee would be able to keep about 35 cents (see figure 4.3).

And again, that's a best-case scenario in which Mary got a high-paying job and found inexpensive childcare. If she were like many men and women who work in parts of the country where taxes, childcare, and other expenses are moderately high but wages only average or low, Mary could face a net loss in going to work. Couples in this situation must decide whether their work is important enough to "pay" for the privilege of doing it.

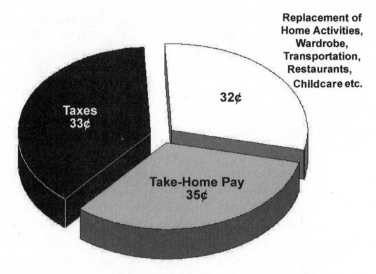

**FIGURE 4.3.** Take-Home Pay (for a woman married to a middle-income husband)

## Problem No. 3:
## Withdrawal Pains

Every couple in America potentially faces the issue of the marriage penalty, but the tax system exacerbates the problem for those on the two opposite ends of the income spectrum.

As we saw earlier in the case of Trixie, spouses of higher-income earners (like Ed) face extremely high marginal rates because their spouse's income pushes them into very high tax brackets. And an unintended consequence is that many lower-earning spouses choose not to work.

Because it is often women who are the lower earners in these higher income families, the tax system has the biggest effect on women's basic life choices, including whether they can afford to pursue a career. This in turn brings up some thorny social issues. Many Americans desire to see the "rich" pay more in taxes. But they might not feel that way if they knew that the tax system keeps many motivated and productive women from making valuable contributions to our economy.

The problem of high marginal tax rates is not only a burden for high-income couples. At the other end of the income scale, low-income earners face very high marginal rates, for a different reason: the withdrawal of tax subsidies and welfare benefits as they earn higher wages.

Consider a single mother who works but still qualifies for a number of government aid programs such as food stamps, Medicaid, and perhaps even cash assistance. This woman falls in love with a man and gets married, full of dreams of a happy, stable home. But then financial realities sink in. The combination of their incomes throws them into a higher tax bracket. The woman no longer qualifies for welfare checks, and her eligibility for food stamps dries up. The couple discovers they will receive less in the form of an Earned Income Tax Credit refund, which furnishes money to low-income workers. And if they earn too much to qualify for Medicaid, they must buy expensive private insurance instead. Combining higher marginal tax rates with a withdrawal of benefits, the couple may discover that while they are "earning" more, they are even less able to pay the bills than before.

The welfare reform of the late 1990s did much to encourage and help single mothers to find jobs and break out of a cycle of dependence. But Congress has yet to deal with the problems that higher marginal tax rates cause for low-income families. If anything, the tax law encourages many low-income women not to marry at all, since marriage often makes them financially worse off.

## Problem No. 4: A Lifetime of Working and Taxes

A family's decision about whether both spouses should go to work is a complicated one, at least financially. What we haven't talked about is how these complications work when the effects are viewed over a whole lifetime.

The immediate "good" of going to work is the money we bring home for things we need or want. The immediate "bad" is the amount the government takes out of our wages or the loss of government aid when earning a higher paycheck. Added to all this are various long-term considerations. Working for a paycheck, for instance, tends to increase the Social Security benefits we'll receive in retirement years. On the other hand, it also increases the amount of taxes we pay on those benefits. People who work more tend to save more, say through an IRA or a 401(k) program. But that increased private retirement income could result in higher taxes on the retirement income when it is withdrawn.

Confusing? Yes. In fact, figuring out the net dollar effect of all these goods and bads over a whole life is pretty much humanly impossible without the aid of a sophisticated computer program. Fortunately, Boston University economist Laurence Kotlikoff and Federal Reserve Bank of Cleveland senior economic adviser Jagadeesh Gokhale developed just such a program. Their results suggest that the minute a two-earner couple begins to earn a decent income (which isn't hard to do), the bads begin to outweigh the goods.

Kotlikoff and Gokhale discovered that, when you figure taxes and lost benefits over a *lifetime*, the current system is onerously stacked against two-earner households. And this reality is most pronounced for low-income families on the verge of moving into a more stable middle-class life. What does a low-income couple gain from a wife's decision to go to work? To answer this question, Kotlikoff and Gokhale calculated marginal net tax rates (the lifetime penalty in terms of taxes and lost benefits).[4]

If the wife of a husband earning $20,000 a year goes to work and she herself earns $10,000 a year, her marginal net tax rate will be 122 percent! That means for every dollar she earns, the couple will give up $1.22 in increased taxes and reduced benefits.

Although it is a bit unusual for marginal net tax rates to exceed 100 percent, it is not unusual for those rates to exceed 50 percent. Second-earner workers in moderate-income families typically lose half of all they earn to higher taxes and lost transfer benefits when all their years of work are taken into consideration (see figure 4.4).

The seminal work of Kotlikoff and Gokhale shows that in order to be truly fair to dual-earner couples we need to do much more than just change the income tax system. We also need to overhaul Social Security and our entire approach to welfare and other government aid programs. We'll discuss these public policy issues in greater detail in chapters to come.

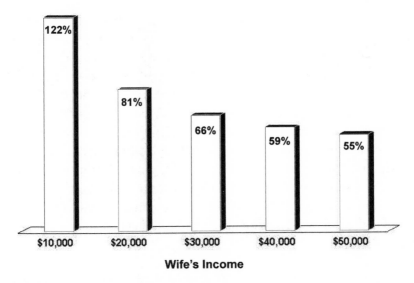

**FIGURE 4.4.** Lifetime Marginal Net Tax Rates for a Woman Whose Husband Earns $20,000 a Year. (Source: Jagadeesh Gokhale and Laurence Kotlikoff, "Does It Pay Both Spouses to Work?" NCPA Policy Report No. 260, May 2003, Figure I)

## WHAT CAN BE DONE?

Millions of Americans face an added tax burden for no other reason than the fact that they got married and have careers. This bias against two-earner couples primarily exists because the lower earner in any home is taxed at rates of the higher-earning spouse, which can discourage careers if not marriage itself.

The most straightforward way to solve this problem is to tax all income at the same rate, regardless of who earns it. Two different proposals for doing this have been gaining steam in America and in other countries. The most talked about is a flat tax. Under that system, both spouses would be taxed at the same marginal rate, regardless of their earnings. So, a couple earning a combined $30,000 would pay, say, 15 percent of that income, while a $200,000 a year couple would pay 15 percent of theirs.[5] High-income earners would pay more total taxes but they would pay the same flat rate as low-income earners.

The other proposal is a national sales tax. Such a system would tax consumption, or what we buy, much in the way state sales taxes do now.[6] High-income earners would spend more and pay more taxes, while lower-income earners would spend less and pay less tax—but all would pay the same rate. So, like a flat tax, couples wouldn't be punished by virtue of being married.

Of course, creating either of those systems means a complete overhaul of the American tax system. But there are other, less radical, ways of making tax life easier for married people. One solution would be to revert to a system under which individuals are truly taxed as separate entities and do not have to combine their incomes. At the very least we could give couples the option of being taxed together or filing as separate individuals.[7]

# WOMEN AND HEALTH

D ANIELLE COUNTS herself fortunate because she started her career at a newspaper that offered a fairly comprehensive health-care plan. When she left in 2002 to attend journalism school in New York, she had her health care covered by the university. It was only when she graduated in the spring of 2003 that health care became a problem.

At the beginning of her time as a freelance journalist she tried doggedly to find coverage. She got in touch with her undergraduate university in Ohio to see if they offered a plan for graduates. They did, but because of state laws she wasn't allowed to use it in New York. She went online to apply for different plans but received only one quote back. Her graduate school offered a federal COBRA plan,[1] but it would have cost $900 for three months—far more than she could afford at the time. She did finally locate a journalist organization that offered plans but even the cheapest was $230 a month—still more than she was able to pay.

One of the things that struck Danielle as she looked was just how much it costs to obtain health insurance independently. Whereas her previous employer had provided her insurance as a tax-free benefit, Danielle was faced with having to first pay taxes on all she earned and then use what was left to buy fairly expensive insurance. She was also disturbed that she couldn't find any plans that offered basic coverage for a healthy

31-year-old. "All I wanted was something that would cover me in case I needed to go the emergency room—something that ran $50 or $100 a month. I didn't need more than that." Unable to locate anything suitable, she decided to risk it and go without insurance until she found a full-time job.

It didn't take long for Danielle to discover how frightening this decision could be. "I was crossing the street in New York, and I wasn't paying much attention and a car was blocking my view," she explained. Next thing she knew she'd been hit by another vehicle. She flew up on its hood and tumbled off the side as she watched the car speed away. Danielle was fortunately able to pick herself up and get home. She wanted to go to the hospital, but knew from experience that emergency rooms could be expensive. "I was living from paycheck to paycheck and worried that an ER bill would be more than I could afford." Luckily, her roommate was in his third year of medical residency and was able to reassure her that nothing was seriously wrong.

Since then, Danielle has obtained a job at a public relations firm. The good news is that she has a choice of four different health plans. Yet because her new plan is different from those offered by her graduate school, she had to find new doctors. Danielle has also looked into other options, such as putting money into a special health-savings account. But the plan she examined requires her to decide one year at a time on a payroll deduction, and if she makes the wrong guess about her likely health expenses, she has to forfeit any funds left in the account at year-end. So she can't see the point. "I can't make a decision in November about what my health needs are going to be for exactly 12 months," she says.

Anyone who has been prescribed a course of antibiotics by the family doctor, had their eyes checked, been to the emergency room, or dealt with a chronic illness knows that our health system is facing some serious challenges. It was conceived in an age when medicine was designed to treat accidents or diseases and when most Americans figured they would only live as long as their genes or luck held out. But today's Americans are far more in control of their health destinies. They can eat right and go to the gym, or they can eat all the wrong things and be a couch potato. They also have access to an amazing array of medical innovations to help them live longer and healthier. Modern drugs and procedures can prevent, treat, and cure diseases that our grandparents accepted as a fact of life. This is all fabulous news, save one thing: These wonders cost money.

In contrast to most developed countries, America's health system is largely private. Precisely because our private health-care system is decentralized and competitive, Americans aren't subject to long waits and outdated technology as are citizens in countries with national health insurance.[2] On the other hand, our employer-based system hasn't kept step with our increasingly mobile and dynamic labor market.

In this chapter we'll look at some of the biggest challenges of today's system. Although the problems affect us all, they take their biggest toll on women. Mothers and wives tend to make most of the decisions about health care for their families, and women are ultimately responsible for 60 percent of spending in the medical marketplace.[3] One polling firm put it best by noting, "While men read about healthcare, women live it every day."[4]

And while it's common knowledge that men tend to die younger than women, women still use far more health care.[5] One-third of women between the ages of 18 and 64 are subject to a chronic health condition requiring medical treatment, compared with 26 percent of men. Half of all women take at least one prescription drug on a regular basis, compared with 31 percent of men.[6] All told, women account for 61 percent of the 700 million doctors' office visits each year and two-thirds of the 44 million hospital visits annually.

Women, as a result, have a greater stake in a system that keeps costs under control and in insurance plans with coverage that meets their needs. While women have health insurance to about the same extent as men, they have less choice. Some 27 percent of females get insurance through someone else, usually at their husband's place of work.[7] When companies scale back employee benefits to cut costs (which they frequently do), or when a husband retires and goes on Medicare, wives are left without any coverage—and often at vulnerable times in their lives.

Women are also more affected by insurance that is not portable. As we mentioned in previous chapters, women comprise the most dynamic and mobile portion of the labor market. They tend to stay in their jobs for shorter periods of time than men, dropping out to care for children or families. Yet they are unable to take their health plans with them, leading to disruptions in care. Many are in industries that offer meager or no health benefits at all.[8] And because they are at greater risk of being uninsured, women are also hurt more by the lack of a national social safety net.

### PROBLEM NO. 1:
### THE DREADED DOCTOR BILL

For most Americans, the very thought of getting, keeping, and using health care is enough to bring on an emergency-room-sized migraine. At the top of the list of worries is cost. And women get hit with these headaches more than men. The Kaiser Family Foundation reports that women consistently worry about their health care more than men and that their highest priority is to make health care more affordable.[9]

Despite these worries, most of us have no idea how much we are already paying for health care. The nation's total health-care bill is nearly $1.6 trillion a year—far higher than the GDP of many countries. That trillion-plus figure averages out to more than $5,000 for every man, woman, and child in the country—or $20,000 a year for a family of four. Since the average family's actual expenses are only a fraction of that amount, most of us are paying an enormous amount of money for other people's sniffles, surgeries, and medication as well as for their long-term care.

If those figures come as a complete surprise to you, there's a good reason. The real costs of health care are hidden from view. For instance, close to half the nation's health-care bills are paid by the government. Medicare pays medical expenses for the elderly and the disabled. Medicaid looks after the poor, the disabled, and indigent nursing home residents. All the money for these programs comes out of our taxes, of course. But since our tax forms don't include helpful line items showing just how much of our money goes to health care (or to anything else, for that matter), few people realize how much of their tax dollars goes to health care. If we *were* able to add it up, it would show that most of us are paying more in taxes for other people's health care and health insurance than we are paying for our own.

People who obtain health care from their workplace aren't much better informed about those costs. As noted earlier, economists view paying for employee health care as an alternative to paying workers more in wages. So employer payments are really coming out of the employees' pockets. But how much are employers actually shelling out for our health care? According to the Bureau of Labor Statistics, the average cost of employee health benefits for 2002 was $3,060 for a single employee and $7,954 for a family.[10]

If you have employer-provided health insurance for your family, chances are you are racking up a lot less than $7,954 of medical expenses each year—unless someone in your family has a serious illness. Since this is money that the company is putting into a health plan instead of into your paycheck, many of us are again handing over a significant amount of money each year for someone else's medical woes.

In one sense this is how health insurance is supposed to work. We all pay premiums into a pool, and only those who get sick draw money out. Health insurance, like life insurance, is a gamble you want to lose. If you are cashing in, it usually means something is seriously wrong.

The question is: Are we getting our money's worth for the dollars we spend? Unfortunately, the answer for most of us is no. But the good news is that there is a way of getting better value, as we will show.

## Problem No. 2:
## You Can't Take It with You

Back in the *Pleasantville* days, health care was pretty straightforward. The husband went to work and with his job came health insurance. If he or anyone in his family fell sick, they could go to any doctor of their choosing or enter any hospital they liked, and their company's insurance plan paid most of the bills.

If the husband switched jobs, chances were that his family could continue seeing the same doctors, since his new employer's insurance would work the same way as the previous one. Such a system—in which employees make all the choices and insurance companies write all the checks—is known as "fee for service," and it was the primary way of doing things when most employers first started offering health insurance.

Things aren't so easy in the age of managed care, where each employer plan tends to have its own network of hospitals and doctors, and its own sets of rules. In this environment, if employees switch jobs, they'll probably have to switch health plans as well, which means searching for new physicians and facilities. If anyone in the family has a health problem, this can mean an interruption in crucial care. And since different companies offer different benefits, an employee may find that coverage for a medical condition under one employer's plan is not available in a new job.

These disruptions are a direct consequence of tying health benefits to a specific place of work. For the majority of us who are healthy most of the time, a change in a health plan may only amount to minor inconveniences. But for families with ongoing health problems—who may have spent years building up trust in a specific doctor or who depend on a specific facility to provide a specialized treatment—the disruption can be life altering. Many employees end up working away at jobs they don't like or want for the sole reason of keeping the health-care plan they currently have.

Even then, there's no guarantee that a worker won't have her health plan snatched out from beneath her feet. Nearly all employer health insurance contracts only run for 12 months at a time. At the end of the year, the employer—often searching for a way to reduce costs—may choose a different health plan. Or the company may decide to quit providing health insurance altogether. The irony is that while many people believe the safest type of health insurance is employer-provided, the only people with health insurance guaranteed to last more than one year are those who purchase it on their own.

The big reason companies continue to give their workers health insurance rather than pay them higher wages (with which, for instance, they could buy their own plans) is tax law. The government grants huge tax advantages for benefits obtained through an employer—tax advantages that are off-limits to people who purchase insurance on their own.

But just because employers foot all or most of the premium doesn't mean health insurance needs to be company-specific. Why can't employees enroll in health plans that meet their needs and stay in those plans as they travel from job to job? Such a system, known as *personal and portable health insurance*, would solve many of the problems. Getting to such a system, however, will first involve a major overhaul of federal policies.

## PROBLEM NO. 3:
## CHOICE IS NOT AN OPTION

One drawback to employer-provided insurance is the potential for disruption. There's also another difficulty: employees are usually stuck with the health plan their company gives them rather than one they would prefer. Estimates of the number of insured employees today who have no choice of health plans range from 42 to 60 percent.[11] A further 12 to 18 percent of insured workers are offered a choice of only two plans.[12] This lack of choice is completely at odds with the larger world of insurance, where diversity is the order of the day.

At one end of the spectrum are *health maintenance organizations*. Members of HMOs can obtain almost all services without opening their wallets, but they must agree to see only the HMO's doctors and get treated only at the HMO's facilities. The upside of HMOs is that they take care of most of the bills. The downside is that they call all the shots, making most decisions for the patients and limiting their options.

At the other extreme are those traditional *fee-for-service* plans, which are becoming as rare as Model T Fords. These plans give patients the most choice, allowing them to see any doctor or receive treatment in any facility. The tradeoff is that fee-for-service plans cost more, and often require substantial out-of-pocket payments before insurance kicks in.

In between these two end posts are *preferred-provider organizations*. PPOs will pay all or most of the bills if patients agree to stick with doctors and facilities in the PPO network. Enrollees are usually allowed to go out of the network, but must pay more out of pocket if they do.

Typically there's also a lot of choice *within* each of these worlds. A family shopping for private insurance might choose one HMO over another because of the good reputation of that particular network's pediatricians. A young couple thinking of having children might choose a PPO that has slightly higher premiums than others but which offers the most expansive prenatal coverage. A young, healthy individual may choose a fee-for-service plan that has low premiums but a high deductible (rather than the other way around) because she knows that there is only a small likelihood she'll have to see a doctor in the course of the year.

Yet while all of these options exist in principle, they are beyond the reach of the many Americans who work for single-plan companies. And while employers may end up providing an insurance plan that is good for many or most of its employees, no single health plan is likely to meet the needs of all workers.

Nor do employers have an interest in solving every employee's health problems. Sure, it is smart business to offer health insurance good enough to attract employees. But this is only true to a point. Companies that offer great health benefits also risk attracting employees (and their families) who have expensive medical problems. In just one example we know of, a father accepted a job in the mailroom of a large company (a job for which he was way overqualified) for the sole purpose of obtaining several hundred thousand dollars of annual benefits for his child's very rare health condition.

A single employee can significantly boost a company's overall expenses. Companies understand these risks and in order to avoid extraordinary costs, they may elect to offer less generous health plans. Critics may blame employers for not being more generous. But a more rational way of looking at it is to see that so long as employers are providing insurance, they are unlikely to satisfy the needs of every employee. The employer's job is to weigh costs and benefits and to run the business efficiently. That goal isn't necessarily in keeping with providing the best health insurance for all employees.

Women have a large stake in a smarter system that offers more choice. Finding a health plan that works is obviously a concern for both sexes. But women have a greater interest in finding doctors who meet their needs.[13] Women are more likely to be undertreated and misdiagnosed, for example. Among patients hospitalized for coronary heart disease, women are less likely to receive angiograms, angioplasty, or bypass graphs than men. They are also more often inappropriately treated for pain.[14] One way to cure these deficiencies is to give women more choice, both *within* plans and *among* plans.

## PROBLEM NO. 4:
## THE CONTROLLING FACTOR

Imagine a young woman who steps out of the shower and notices a small mole on her arm that was never there before. It doesn't hurt; it doesn't look unhealthy. But her mother had melanoma and soon the woman begins to worry about skin cancer. She goes in to see her HMO doctor, who gives the mole a look, says it probably isn't anything to worry about, and tells her to wait and see if it gets bigger. The woman says she'd feel better if he ordered a biopsy. But her doctor says that since the spot doesn't look problematic, the HMO won't authorize such a diagnostic test. The young woman goes on worrying.

Of all the problems with managed care, the biggest one is that a nameless and faceless bureaucracy scoops up all the health-care dollars while also making many treatment decisions. In a day and age when medical science has more and more to offer, managed care is still calling all the shots for many patients—with decisions often based on how best to cut costs. And although doctors are ethically bound to put their patients' interests first, many tend to view employers or health insurers, rather than the patients, as their real customers. It is only human nature to be influenced by the people who write the checks.

It's no surprise then that some of the biggest arguments in health care come down to differences over what patients feel they deserve and what managed care companies feel they should have to deliver. A good example is disputes over diagnostic tests, much like the one our fictional young woman wanted to have for the mole on her arm.

In an old-fashioned fee-for-service world, this woman would be freer to make her own decisions about the number and types of tests she receives. Some patients might run off to have a biopsy done on every mole—just so that they don't have to worry. Others might wait to see if the spot bothers them before they see a doctor. The problem is: The woman who wants a biopsy for her mole is forcing everyone else in her insurance plan to pay for her peace of mind. That's why old-fashioned insurance has become so expensive that few of us can afford it.

Things are different in the managed care world. Because HMOs pay all the bills (or rather all those paying into the plan pay all the bills), the organization has an interest in discouraging patients from overconsuming health care. Managed care, as a result, tends to be one-size-fits-all; impersonal guidelines tend to dictate the right number of tests for every circumstance, regardless of patient preferences.

One of the most fascinating examples of one-size-fits-all controversy happened nearly a decade ago when Hillary Rodham Clinton took on the country's health-care system. Clinton's idea was to create a new health-care system based on the principles of managed care, and one job of her task force was to define a package of benefits every American should have, down to the smallest detail.

Most of the task force's recommendations were directed at broad changes. But oddly enough it was the group's recommendations about the little things—such as the frequency of diagnostic tests—that caused a real firestorm. The Clinton task force, for instance, recommended regular mammograms for women in their fifties but not for those in their forties. For sexually active young women, the task force recommended a Pap smear every third year, rather than every year or every other year— as most doctors were recommending at the time.[15] The uproar helped to doom the task force's plans.

### Thinking about Preventive Care

Controversy aside, the Clinton task force was on to something when it came to diagnostic tests. It recognized an important truth about preventive care.

Most people mistakenly believe that diagnostic tests and other types of preventive care tend to save money. More often than not, that's simply not the case.[16] Yes, catching a woman's breast cancer early is likely to lower the cost of her treatment. But in order to identify the one woman who has cancer, health organizations have to give mammograms to thousands of healthy patients. Get out the calculator, and you will find that the extra costs of screening all those healthy women add up to far more than the reduced costs of early treatment for the few who have the disease.

Studies have shown over and over that preventive care usually costs us far more money than it saves. Consider a few reports that were done about the same time the Clinton task force was meeting. The studies looked at the cost of screening (including the costs of treatment for those found to have cancer) for every year of life saved as a result of the screening and treatment.

One report, for instance, showed that giving regular mammograms to women aged 55 to 64 costs about $110,000 for every year of life saved as a result of the screening, when all costs are considered. Giving the same regular mammograms to women in their forties, however, caused costs to jump up to $190,000 for each year of life saved (see figure 5.1).

Another report found that screening young women every four years for cervical cancer costs less than $12,000 for each year of life saved—considered a very "good buy" in the business of risk avoidance. But what happens when the exams are administered more frequently? Giving women cervical exams every three years costs $220,000 for each year of life saved. The number hit $310,000 at two-year intervals. And giving a Pap smear to women every year costs $1.5 million per year of life saved (see figure 5.2).

The mistake the Clinton task force made wasn't to factor in these costs and benefits in attempting to figure out what would give health care

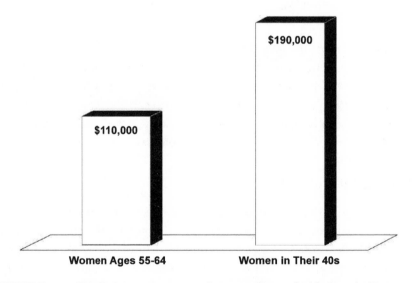

**FIGURE 5.1.** Yearly Mammograms: Cost per Year of Life Saved. (Source: Tammy O. Tengs et al., "Five-Hundred Life-Saving Interventions and Their Cost-Effectiveness," *Risk Analysis*, Vol. 15, No. 3, June 1995)

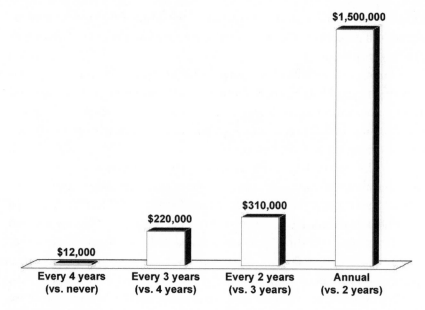

**FIGURE 5.2.** Cervical Cancer Tests: Cost Per Life-Year Saved (women, age 20). (Source: Tammy O. Tengs et al., "Five-Hundred Life-Saving Interventions and Their Cost-Effectiveness," *Risk Analysis*, Vol. 15, No. 3, June 1995)

the most bang for its buck. That's what all of us do naturally. We tend to weigh risks and benefits when deciding how to spend our money.[17]

No, the real mistake the Clinton task force made was thinking that it was the White House's job to make the same decisions for every American. People are different. Their attitudes toward risks are different. And there is no reason why we must all make the same choices.

## Making Individual Decisions

One-size-fits-all decisions occur because managed care puts all its eggs into one financial basket. Since the insurer must approve the spending of all the health-care dollars, it has a responsibility to make sure that one person's hypochondria doesn't waste the premium contributions of others.

This problem isn't unique to health care. But in other insurance markets, insurers long ago realized it doesn't make financial sense to insure for all contingencies. A good example is automobile casualty insurance.

Americans take for granted that they will self-insure (pay themselves) for all the routine maintenance and other occasional repairs to their cars. Such a system encourages each of us to make prudent cost-benefit decisions about the basics, such as changing the oil and aligning the tires. Yet we can have an insurance backstop in case something really bad happens.

We need something equivalent in the health-care industry. One solution is to give people a fund from which they can pay for their own routine, personal health-care decisions, rather than letting an insurance company control all the health-care dollars. Mammograms are a good example. Some 10 years after the Clinton task force fell apart, experts still can't agree on the importance of mammograms.[18] It could be years, or decades, before that puzzle is solved. In the meantime, some women need a way to pay for the exams for their own peace of mind while not increasing costs for everyone else.

Ditto cervical cancer tests. At a whopping $1.5 million per year of life saved, it's socially impossible to justify giving every young woman an annual Pap smear. The payoff is too low, especially considering all the health benefits that might otherwise come from a wiser use of money. But allowing women to make their own decisions, with their own funds, is a different matter. Most diagnostic tests cost a few hundred dollars or less. If having a test allows a patient to sleep better at night, the personal cost might be worth the personal benefit.

And there's a further reason for giving people access to personal accounts and more control over their health-care dollars. Health plans are increasingly allowing their members to go to out-of-network doctors and facilities—where the patients must spend more out of their own pockets. In fact, 34 states *require* that health plans let their enrollees go out of network.[19]

Congress is considering the same type of legislation at the federal level. Yet what use will all this choice be if patients don't have the financial ability to use it?

Having a personal medical account to pay expenses would be a special boon to women. Studies show that among people with employer-provided insurance, women spend 68 percent more out of pocket than men.[20] And women without such accounts are also more likely to forgo care because of worries about costs.[21]

## Problem No. 5:
## Saying No to Self-Insurance

How do we get to a system in which people have more control over their own health-care money and their own health-care decisions? The first step is to get rid of a federal tax bias against self-insurance.

There are two basic ways to insure against risky events. One is to shift all the risk to a third-party insurer and pay premiums to cover the costs. The other is to self-insure, by setting aside money to pay for things as and when they happen. As discussed earlier, normal insurance markets deal naturally with these two options. People tend to use outside insurers for those big, risky events over which they have little control and cost a lot, while self-insuring for less risky events that generate small costs and over which they have more control. Unfortunately, health care isn't a normal insurance market.

The problem is federal tax law. Consider a middle-income technology worker. Currently, every dollar her employer pays to Blue Cross/Blue Shield in premiums is a dollar of benefits on which she, the tech worker, doesn't have to pay taxes. The health insurance she receives is tax-free. But if her company were to deposit, say, $100 a month into an account from which she could pay some of her own medical expenses, she'd have to fork over 25 percent in federal income taxes and 5 percent in state income taxes (depending on her tax bracket), as well as another 7.65 percent in FICA payroll taxes. Before she's even spent a dime on a diagnostic test, she will have given more than one-third of her new medical funds to the government.

Tax policy, in other words, smiles benevolently on third-party insurance but frowns severely on those who self-insure. Naturally, we all adjust to the tax code. Most of us have the type of health insurance we have because that's what the tax law encourages.

Thankfully, Congress has acknowledged the need for innovation and has so far allowed three important exceptions to the general rule.

### Flexible Spending Accounts

Under flexible spending accounts (FSAs), employers and their employees can both make pretax deposits. People can use the money in their accounts to pay for medical expenses that aren't covered by the company's health plan. With an FSA, women can pay for those tests and other extras that they view as important to their health, even though the employer's plan won't pay for them. Some health plans, for instance, don't cover prescribed contraceptives. But with an FSA, workers can buy them with pretax dollars. Likewise, women who use their FSA money for annual mammograms, Pap smears, or other preventive measures would get the same tax benefits they would have if their company had paid for these services via insurance premiums.

FSAs aren't perfect. Their main drawback is that they are governed by a use-it-or-lose-it rule. Employees who don't use all the money by the end of the year have to forfeit the balance. This leads to all sorts of perverse behavior. At the end of the year, employees rush out to buy expensive new eyeglasses or purchase other items they don't really need, because it's that or nothing. FSAs are therefore better described as "spending accounts," rather than "saving accounts." Congress could fix this defect with a simple change in the law that would allow workers to roll over their unspent balances into the next year. FSAs would then become a genuine form of self-insurance.[22]

## Medical Savings Accounts

Another exception to the rule is an innovative pilot program started in 1996. Under the program, the self-employed and employees of small businesses could purchase high-deductible insurance and pay for expenses below the deductible from a Medical Savings Account (MSA). MSAs were a great success for the people who had them. But the rules that governed the MSA program were so restrictive that most Americans had difficulty getting access.[23]

## Health Savings Accounts

To remedy this problem, a new law replaces MSAs with Health Savings Accounts (HSAs), which in principle are now available to all nonelderly Americans. HSAs work like this: Third-party insurance usually pays for all expenses above a high deductible—say $1,000 for an individual or

$2,000 for a family. The employee has to cover all the expenses below the deductible, but her employer can make deposits to the HSA to help cover some, or all, of their deductible expenses. And unlike FSAs, any balance left at the end of the year rolls over to the next and grows tax free—just like an IRA or 401(k) account.[24]

The experience of other countries shows that HSAs can make a great contribution to health-care markets. South Africa under Nelson Mandela, for instance, allowed HSA-type plans to develop in a relatively free, private health system. Today, these plans represent more than half the market for private insurance in the country.[25]

### Health Reimbursement Arrangements

Health Reimbursement Arrangements (HRAs) is an experimental program that shows great promise. With HRAs, a company makes chunks of money available for each worker—say, $500 or $1,000. Unlike FSAs, the money can be rolled over from year to year, making it a true health "savings" account. Companies can also make the balance available to employees even when they leave the company, allowing them to purchase their own health care or pay health insurance premiums.[26] The only drawback is that employees cannot take the balance as cash and use it for items other than health care.

All of these programs—FSAs, MSAs, HSAs, and HRAs—are a first step in allowing people to self-insure for routine health care. They also give workers far more control over their health-care decisions. All head in the direction of a significantly reformed health-care system.

## Problem No. 6:
## Saying No to Individually Owned Insurance Too

For the most part, we've dealt with the trials and tribulations of employees at companies that provide health insurance. But insurance can also be daunting for workers who purchase their own. And once again, the problems begin with the tax code.

The federal government, as noted in figure 5.3, heavily subsidizes employer-provided health insurance via taxes. For a middle-class family,

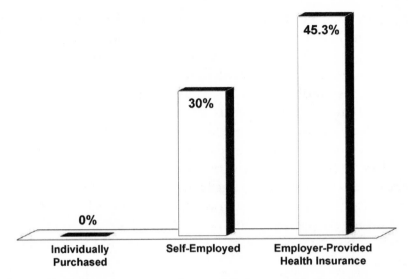

**FIGURE 5.3.** Federal and State Tax Subsidies for Private Insurance. Note: Assumes taxpayer is in the 25 percent federal income tax bracket, faces a 15.3 percent payroll (FICA) tax and a 5 percent state and local income tax.

the subsidy is roughly equal to about half of the premium cost. This means that if you happen to work at a big company with benefits, the federal government is already paying for half of the cost of your health insurance.[27]

But the government gets a lot more tight-fisted when it comes to helping people who purchase their own insurance. While the tax code allows people who are self-employed to write off 100 percent of their health insurance, this relief is much less than what a similarly situated person would receive if the insurance were purchased through an employer.[28] And people who aren't self-employed but who purchase their own health insurance get virtually no help whatsoever.[29]

This lack of tax aid can make a huge difference to a family's bottom line. Consider someone like Danielle, who was facing a $2,500-a-year premium as a freelancer. When Danielle worked at the newspaper, her employer took $2,500 of what would otherwise be her wages and used that pretax money to pay insurance premiums. But when Danielle went out on her own, she had to earn almost twice that sum in order to be able to pay the taxes and buy the insurance with what's leftover. In this sense, people who buy their own insurance have to pay twice as much.

That tax penalty becomes particularly burdensome for women who are inching toward retirement. Many women are married to older men. Yet when their husbands retire and qualify for Medicare, wives are no longer covered by their husbands' employer health plans. At the same time, Medicare won't allow members to sign up underage spouses. Until the wife hits 65 and can also enroll in Medicare, she'll have to purchase her own insurance with after-tax dollars. She'll also be at a time in her life when she's charged higher premiums for health insurance, since health risks tend to rise with age. And she'll pay even more (or possibly even be denied insurance altogether) if she already has an expensive health problem or is recovering from a disease such as breast cancer.

The more one looks at the way the tax system treats health insurance, the more unfair it seems. For instance, the current tax code tends to give the most generous health tax breaks to those who need them the least.[30] Government tax subsidies for private health insurance currently total a staggering $141 billion a year. Further, on the average, families who earn $100,000 a year or more get about six times as much tax relief as families who earn only $25,000 (see figure 5.4).

That isn't to say that we should be subsidizing lower-income families more than higher-income families. There's a much better argument for simply giving the same insurance tax break to one and all, rich or poor.

Why? Step back and ask yourself why the government should encourage people to buy health insurance in the first place. The usual argument is that one person's failure to insure ends up costing all the rest of us.[31] At a time of a serious illness, the uninsured are still likely to get health care—even if they aren't insured. Everyone else ends up paying for much of the cost through higher taxes, higher premiums, or higher medical bills (as costs are shifted from those who don't pay to those who do).

This argument, moreover, doesn't just apply to families with low incomes. A family earning $100,000 a year can incur hospital costs that it cannot pay almost as easily as a family that earns $25,000 a year. For this reason, government efforts to encourage private insurance should be about the same, regardless of income.

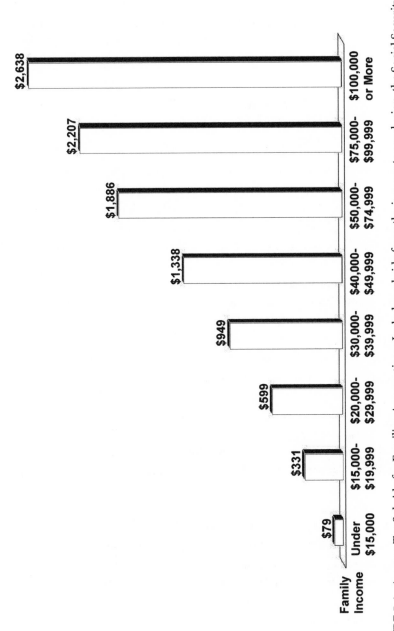

**FIGURE 5.4.** Average Tax Subsidy for Families. Assumptions: Includes subsidy from the income tax exclusion, the Social Security payroll tax exclusion, and the health expenses deduction. (Source: John Sheils, Paul Hogan, and Randall Haught, "Health Insurance and Taxes: The Impact of Proposed Changes in Current Federal Policy," National Coalition on Health Care, October 18, 1999)

What we really need is a level playing field, not just between rich and poor but also between different types of insurance users. Government should be granting just as much tax relief to those who purchase their own insurance as it grants to those who obtain insurance through an employer.

## PROBLEM NO. 7: UNINSURED AND LOVING IT

High costs. Perverse tax laws. Lack of choice and control. The average person might wonder why she should go to all the effort to get insured. Even more so if she looks around and discovers that many Americans receive health care without going through all the hassle. These "many Americans" are the uninsured, and their ranks are growing.

That America has a real problem with the uninsured was never clearer than in the 1990s. Economists usually expect to see more people sign up for private insurance during times of economic plenty. But despite the 1990s boom—and the fact that managed care was reasonably successful during that time at holding down insurance costs—the percentage of the population that was uninsured kept right on climbing. Driving the trend numbers are three perverse public policies that actually encourage many people to go without coverage.

### Free Care

Most of the uninsured are people who don't work for an employer who provides the tax-subsidized benefits we mentioned earlier.[32] So they face the prospect of buying their insurance with after-tax dollars. This, we have seen, can make insurance payments twice as expensive.

At the same time, what do they have to lose from *not* getting insurance? They may receive a stack of medical bills in the mail that they can't pay. But not being able to pay a bill is not the same as not getting health care. We are currently spending buckets of money on "free care" for the uninsured. Under federal law, hospital emergency rooms can't turn away patients who don't have insurance.[33] And most states and communities offer a raft of programs that help provide free care to the uninsured, many of them funded with federal tax dollars.[34]

Just how much free care is out there? Take the example of Texas, where a rigorous study by the State Comptroller's Office found that "free" health care amounts to about $1,000 for every uninsured Texas resident every year.[35] That equals $4,000 for a family of four—enough to buy good private insurance in many Texas cities.

Let's imagine for a moment the choices available to a Texas family of four. The parents can work to obtain $8,000 hard-earned dollars to pay for both taxes and private insurance. Or, they can rely on the $4,000-per-family free care system offered by the public sector. It's hard to blame families for choosing to bank on the social safety net.

Texas is not alone. An Urban Institute study concludes that other states are equally generous.[36] Overall, public policy rewards families who hang up on the insurance salesman's calls, even as it penalizes people who buy their own insurance.

What we need, at a minimum, is a neutral government policy, one that at least doesn't encourage people to be uninsured. A way to do this would be to offer people the same amount of dollars to buy their own private insurance as we currently offer them in free health care. We'll go into this in further detail below.

## Government Health Insurance

Another way that public policy encourages people to forgo insurance is through expansion of government insurance, principally Medicaid and the State Children's Health Insurance Programs (SCHIP).

As huge and costly as these programs are (Medicaid for the poor now costs about as much as Medicare for the elderly), their impact is even larger. That's because there are about 13 million Americans who are eligible to enroll, but just haven't bothered to sign up. Many of them could obtain private coverage, say, through an employer. But since they know the government program is there as a backup, they have no incentive to do so.

Imagine a Texas woman who is eligible for Medicaid, but has never signed up and also has no private insurance. She gets in a car accident, incurs thousands of dollars of medical bills, and then is released. After that, she then has three whole months in which to go sign up for Medicaid and have that program pay her hospital bills! Why would anyone purchase private insurance (or pay premiums to an employer plan) if she knows she can always turn to Medicaid or SCHIP?

These programs also have a big influence on employer behavior. If a firm knows that many or most of its employees are eligible for free health insurance, it will also know that health benefits will be viewed as far less valuable than wages by its employees. During the latter part of the 1990s, private insurance coverage of children eligible for SCHIP decreased at almost the same rate that SCHIP expanded its coverage (see figure 5.5). So public insurance was crowding out private insurance. And even though taxpayers were hit with a hefty new expense, the total number of uninsured stayed roughly the same.

Between 1996 and 1999, public coverage for poor children rose four percentage points, while the rate of private health insurance fell by five percentage points, and between 2000 and 2003 public coverage rose

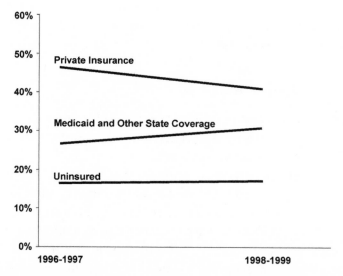

**FIGURE 5.5.** Health Insurance Coverage of Low-Income Children. Note: 5 percent in 1996-1997 and 6 percent in 1998-1999 had other public coverage such as Indian Health Services. (Source: Peter J. Cunningham and Michael H. Park, "Tracking Recent Changes in Health Coverage for Low-Income Children with the Community Tracking Study, 1996-1997 and 1998-1999," Center for Studying Health System Change, Research Report No. 04, April 2000)

roughly nine percentage points while private coverage fell eight per-centage points.[37] Taxpayers paid a lot more, but coverage of children barely budged.

### After-the-Fact Insurance

A third way in which public policy is encouraging people to be uninsured is through federal and state laws that force insurance companies to pro-vide people with coverage for illnesses they already have. Why pay pre-miums when you are healthy, if you know you can always enroll after you get sick?

One nasty side effect of these "guaranteed issue" laws is that they encourage healthy families who could well afford to buy their own insur-ance to go without. Ironically, a growing number of the uninsured are nowhere near poor. In the past few years most of the new entrants into the world of the uninsured have been families who earn more than $50,000 a year; and more than half of those earn in excess of $80,000 a year.[38] Yet when people can game the system, enrolling and paying pre-miums only after they get sick, insurers end up having to raise premiums for everyone else. Some insurance companies have found the market so wrecked by these new after-the-fact laws that they've pulled up stakes and moved out of states altogether, sometimes leaving previously insured families with no insurance at all.

Even before there was widespread guaranteed issue legislation, Census Bureau surveys found that only about 1 percent of the popula-tion was denied insurance because of a health condition.[39] Yet in order to help this 1 percent, well-meaning legislators have created complete havoc in the market for the other 99 percent. The proof is in the num-bers: The states that have been the most aggressive in making it easier for sick people to obtain insurance are states where the numbers of unin-sured are increasing the fastest.[40]

## PROBLEM NO. 8:
## UNFRIENDLY GOVERNMENT INSURANCE

While many families find it in their financial interest to turn to state-sponsored insurance for their care, that doesn't mean that dealing with the public sector is a picnic. Government insurance is both confusing and unfriendly.

A little history might be in order. The federal government first established Medicaid for low-income families in 1965. Though Congress wrote the law creating the program, the responsibility for actually running it falls to the states. The State Children's Health Insurance Program (SCHIP) was then created in 1997 to expand health insurance for children. Like Medicaid, SCHIP has substantial federal funding but is run by governors and state legislatures.

Each state program is a tangle of bureaucracy and rules that usually proves a challenge to navigate. The biggest problem is that different eligibility requirements for each program means that not all members of the same family qualify for the same health insurance program. Under these conflicting rules, it's quite easy to have a mother on Medicaid, a child on SCHIP, and a father on an employer's plan. All three members of this family could be seeing different doctors, going to different facilities, and filling out different forms.

It would be far cheaper for taxpayers, not to mention much easier for low-income families, if the government simply paid the dependent's share of the premium and enrolled the whole family in the employer plan. But in most states, the rules and regulations make sensible solutions impossible. It is also generally impossible to use Medicaid or SCHIP money to enroll an entire family in any private health plan.

## PROBLEM NO. 9:
### THE TATTERED SOCIAL SAFETY NET

America has a long history of providing indigent care. But this dam is full of cracks, and people are already beginning to slip through.

The traditional way of funding is through what economists call "cross subsidies." Physicians and hospitals overcharged those who could pay, and that extra money was used to pay for the free care that went to others.[41]

But cross subsidies don't work well in the new world of health care. The entire cross-subsidy system is premised on a medical marketplace that is not very competitive, and where patients have limited choices. In a competitive market, it becomes very difficult to overcharge, since any consumer who is overcharged will look for a doctor or hospital that offers a better deal.

Of course, the U.S. health-care system is hardly a model of competition. But during the 1980s and 1990s, managed care injected a bit of healthy rivalry and government churned out pro-competition policies. These baby steps have been enough to begin eroding the cross subsidies that normally paid for indigent care, and that process will only continue.[42]

A second source of safety net funding is government programs. The federal government today provides a dizzying array of more than 40 health-care programs to fund services for the uninsured. One of the largest is the Disproportionate Share Hospital (DSH) payment program, which compensates hospitals that serve an above-average number of indigent patients. But there are also programs for public housing residents, seasonal farm workers, legal immigrants, undocumented immigrants, and all sorts of other groups.[43]

As one might expect, this roster of programs is overlapping, wasteful, and inefficient. And funds tend to go to those special interests with the most clout. For example, indigent care money tends to flow freely to hospitals that have ace Washington lobby teams, but often bypasses primary care doctors and clinics that deliver more efficient care. And even when money goes where it should, politicians are usually only too ready to take a knife to it when budgets get tight.

A third source of funds comes from government programs such as Medicaid and SCHIP. Hospital administrators care a lot about who is enrolled in what program, since that determines how they are paid. But the patients themselves may have no reason to care. At Parkland Hospital in Dallas, Medicaid patients and uninsured patients come through the same emergency room door, see the same doctors, and are admitted to the same rooms. Similarly, at the Children's Hospital next door to Parkland, SCHIP children, Medicaid children, and uninsured children all get the exact same treatment.

What we have, as a result, is a system that is inefficient, underfunded, and subject to rationing. It rarely employs the best doctors or provides the best care. Yet because of the policies we have discussed, growing numbers of Americans are dropping out and relying on a ratty-tatty social safety net.

## A PLAN FOR INSURING THE UNINSURED

Have we depressed you? The uplifting news is that there is a solution to these problems so beautifully simple that it is amazing it wasn't implemented decades ago. It doesn't involve new spending. It doesn't involve throwing sick people into the streets. Yet it will increase choice, improve quality, expand the number of people with private insurance, and shore up funding for those who deliver indigent care.

It starts with combining all our tax and spending programs into one coordinated effort. Let's say the government commits $1,000 to every American (or $4,000 for a family of four) for health insurance. Anyone who obtains private insurance—whether independently or through an employer—could claim that $1,000 in the form of a refundable tax credit. ("Refundable" means you get the money back even if you don't owe taxes.) That $1,000, however, is all the help you get.

People who do not privately insure would still be able to rely on a local safety net. But their $1,000 lump sum would instead be made in a block grant to the local community where they live. Local governments would have the freedom to try any sort of creative care system they liked. They might enroll everyone in a Medicaid-like program. They might contract for care with a private provider. They might even try to run a completely socialized system, a sort of local version of the British National Health Service.

The best part of this plan is that it would allow people to make their own choices and then shift government funds accordingly. Suppose, for example, that everyone in Monroe County, New York, who is currently part of the safety net decides to acquire private insurance. This plan would take the $1,000 for each person that currently goes to the safety net and instead allow individuals to apply it to their insurance premiums.

Suppose instead that everyone in Monroe County who is currently insured decides to become uninsured. They would not receive the tax credit, and would essentially pay $1,000 more in taxes than their peers as a "penalty" for being uninsured. Yet each of their $1,000 lump sums would instead be made available to fund the local safety net.

While simple in concept, this plan would undoubtedly involve complicated decisions in practice. It would also surely face special interest opposition, since so many groups owe their existence to today's flawed system. But with a little open-mindedness, even special interest groups might find they have a lot to gain from a health system that uses health care dollars in the wisest and most efficient way.

## WHAT CAN BE DONE?

While stopping way short of the ideal, President George W. Bush has made a number of proposals that would begin to prod our health-care system in the right direction.[44] The big winner is Health Savings Accounts, which became available to non-elderly Americans in 2004. The President has also proposed a refundable tax credit for those who purchase their own insurance. Adults could claim $1,000 apiece and another $500 per child—up to $3,000 for a low- or moderate-income family.

This is a good start, but much more needs to be done. And while health-care problems take a toll on both males and females, the need to get things right is particularly acute for women. Female patients have a greater interest in surmounting managed care restrictions to obtain diagnostic tests and see specialists. Women are therefore more disadvantaged by the tax code's bias against health-care savings accounts and have more to gain by managing some of their own health-care dollars.

Women move from employer to employer more often than men. This means they would benefit the most from portable insurance. Because women tend to earn lower wages, they are also more likely to be hurt by a tax system that subsidizes insurance based on the worker's tax bracket.

Because they experience more time out of the labor market (say, for children) or are more likely to marry an older spouse who will lose private insurance when he enrolls in Medicare, women have a greater need for tax relief for individually owned health insurance. And because women with children are more likely to rely on a health-care safety net, they need a system that is efficient, reasonable, and makes private insurance options a realistic alternative.

The National Center for Policy Analysis has created a blueprint for how to reform our health-care system in ways that address the problems discussed above.[45] Broadly, we need reforms that will:

- Move as quickly as possible to a system of personal and portable health insurance.
- Give people who must purchase their own health insurance as much tax relief as we give people who obtain insurance from an employer.
- Allow people health-care savings accounts so they can make more of their own health-care decisions and exercise more of their own choices.
- Encourage people enrolled in government health insurance programs to enroll in private insurance instead.
- Encourage people who rely on "free care" from local health-care safety nets to enroll in private insurance instead.

# WOMEN AND EDUCATION

WENDA DUECK, a 49-year-old in Colorado, is much more than just a mother to her three children. She's their teacher. Wenda admits that homeschooling her children—an 18-year-old daughter and two boys aged 14 and 12—wasn't originally the plan. She used to think that people who home-schooled had "fallen off the wagon and hit their heads." But then she and her husband, Ken, a real-estate developer, went to visit some friends in Phoenix who had homeschooled their kids. They were both impressed by the "quality of the children."

The more Wenda looked into homeschooling, the more she was interested. She wasn't particularly thrilled with the local public schools; she had concerns about the quality of the teaching and the lack of parental control over anything that happened in the school environment. She and Ken looked into private education, but considering the cost and the fact that it would be at least a 30-minute drive to a private school, Wenda felt the time and money could be better used for an education she could provide. So when her daughter was four years old, Wenda embarked on homeschooling. "We figured we'd evaluate as we went along and then decide if we'd keep going."

Wenda kept going and has since homeschooled all her children—with great success. The program has allowed her and Ken to give their kids the sort of "well-rounded education" that they both think is so important.

Moreover, the entire family has benefited in unique ways. In 1998, Ken sold his business, and the entire family went on a round-the-world trip for three-and-a-half years. They visited 31 countries, traveling on everything from camels to bicycles to elephants. The adventure was designed as one big teaching lesson. In Guatemala, the family took intensive Spanish lessons and are today all fluent. At any one time, the family carted around 75 to 100 pounds of books, which the kids used for general studies and to learn about places they visited. Wenda would trade the old books in for new ones at stores as they went along.

Clearly this family-provided education has had great results. Their oldest daughter, Lauren, scored in the 99th percentile on her PSAT tests. She and a younger brother, struck by the less privileged people they saw on their world trip, are currently forming a bank that will specialize in micro-lending.

Not, of course, that homeschooling is without trade-offs. Financially, it means that only one spouse can bring home an income. And Wenda notes that she doesn't have the freedom to pop out for a mid-morning break with friends since she's busy teaching. "It's certainly a sacrifice," she says, "but considering all the other options, I really feel it was the best choice."

Many parents today, like Wenda Dueck, feel as though they no longer have real control over, or choice in, our modern public system of education.

In the opening scenes of *Pleasantville*, we see David at his modern, sprawling high school, one of hundreds of kids milling around outside the doors before class. It's almost inconceivable to think of David's mother inserting herself into this enormous, self-contained world or having any role alongside hundreds of different teachers, administrators, rules, and programs.

It didn't used to be this way. In the early part of the 20th century, local boards controlled their neighborhood schools, and these boards derived their strength from the intact families who made up the community. In those days, women volunteered to be "homeroom mothers," putting in hours every week inside the school. Mothers and fathers showed up for their local Parent-Teacher Association meetings and wielded real power over curriculum and school management. Ambitious fathers ran for positions on the school board, slots that often proved launching pads for higher public office. Meanwhile, everyone knew that if children did have to drop out of school early to help out with family finances, they'd find jobs within these stable communities and remain gainfully employed throughout their adult lives.

Driving all this involvement was parents' belief that they had primary responsibility for their children's education. They got to know the local teachers and generally supported whatever discipline was handed out in the classroom. Teachers were mostly women, well-educated and committed types who went into one of the few fields that welcomed them at the time.

Most of the things that made the typical neighborhood school so successful started to disappear after World War II. We've described many of these changes in earlier parts of the book: increasing urbanization and suburbanization, rising divorce rates, more unmarried mothers raising children, new careers opening to women, a highly mobile workforce, and mothers of young children working full-time for wages. Between these changes and the rise of teachers unions, many parents no longer had the time or the power to run schools as they had before.

At the same time, education became all the more important and schools were required to teach more. School dropouts could no longer just go find a job at any local business. Literacy, math, and technical training became must-haves for many jobs. The Russian launch of Sputnik in 1957 set off national worries about our schools' deficiencies in math and science. By 1983 a federal task force had delivered a blistering report on the state of public education. It concluded: "If an unfriendly power had attempted to impose on America the mediocre educational performance that exists today, we might well have viewed it as an act of war."[1]

Yet two decades later, the performance of American students—especially in inner-city schools—is disappointing to say the least. Moreover, these unprepared children are setting off into a world where education and future wages are inextricably linked. Better-educated workers command a wage premium in the labor market, and that premium has shot up over time.[2] By contrast, workers with less than a bachelor's degree account for 82.1 percent of the unemployed.[3]

## WELL-INTENTIONED REFORMS

The good news is that America knows it has a learning disability. Educators and public policy officials have been churning out theories and "solutions" to these problems at amazing speed. The bad news is that most of these "solutions" haven't worked.[4]

The biggest redirection in public education came in 1965, when President Lyndon B. Johnson, as part of his "War on Poverty," shepherded through the Elementary and Secondary Education Act (ESEA). A stunning amount of money ($1 billion was huge in 1965) was directed from Washington to local school districts and forced a radical transformation. Although local control wasn't dismantled, it gave way to an expanding education bureaucracy heavily influenced by powerful teachers' unions.[5]

While the ESEA has undergone many changes over the years, the program's main focus was always desegregation as well as equalizing facilities and programs across income groups. Only recently has it been expected to show that students are actually learning something for all the money that is spent. Urged by President George W. Bush, the 2001 No Child Left Behind Act (funded with $15 billion) insists on standards, testing, and informing the public of the results.[6]

By 2005, for example, all states were required to administer standard tests every year to students in grades three through eight. These tests must be linked to statewide high-quality standards, and the results must be made available for all to see. Every state and the District of Columbia is now rating schools according to whether they make "adequate yearly progress." Some 21 states were ahead of the deadline and conducting their standardized tests by spring 2005. In Colorado, the report card on the performance of every public school in the state is even published in the newspapers.

## PROBLEM NO. 1:
## SCHOOL CHOICE[7]

Contrary to widespread impression, America already has an extensive system of school choice. The problem isn't a lack of options. The problem is that most parents don't have the money, the freedom, or the wheels to take advantage of the choices that currently exist.

Take downtown Dallas, with 79 school districts in its 50-mile radius. Assuming each district has at least two campuses at each grade level, a typical family has a choice of about 158 public schools, as long as the parents can afford to buy a house in any neighborhood and are willing to drive a considerable distance to work.

As it happens, many parents do exactly that. A study by researchers at Southern Methodist University and the Dallas Federal Reserve Bank found that North Dallas houses near higher-ranking elementary schools sold for about 20 percent more than houses near lower-ranking schools. Clearly parents are willing to move to neighborhoods with high-quality schools—and the housing market charges a premium for it.[8]

Dallas attorney H. Martin Gibson conducted an informal survey of housing prices in Highland Park—a wealthy Dallas suburb—that underlines just how much more parents are willing to pay to get their kids into good schools. Although most Highland Park homes are inside the Highland Park Independent School District (HPISD), a few are in the Dallas Independent School District (DISD). Gibson found that, all else equal, homes on the HPISD side of the street sell for 24 percent more than those on the DISD side. Many Highland Park homeowners are paying about $72,000 just for the right to send their children to Highland Park schools.[9]

The problem with this type of school choice is that the parents searching for good schools and safe streets end up contributing to ferocious bidding wars for narrow slices of the housing market. Researchers Elizabeth Warren and Amelia Warren Tyagi found that housing prices for childless couples increased 23 percent between 1983 and 1998. But housing prices for married couples with children shot up 79 percent in the same period—more than three times as much. The consequences of this housing inflation can be dire. In order to get into desirable neighborhoods, both parents often take on demanding jobs to pay the mortgage. In some cases they stretch themselves too thin and end up in bankruptcy.[10]

How does the system work for those parents who don't have the resources to buy homes close to good schools? What happens to families who don't even own a car? For the most part, they're out of luck. Since most of what passes as "school choice" throughout America is based on the housing market, it follows that most children in low-income families end up in schools that no one else wants to attend. These are the schools with the worst teachers, the worst principals, and the lowest test scores.

Fortunately, America has been experimenting with some new education options that hold out the hope of real "choice" for many of these lower-income families. What follows is a rundown of some of these exciting new opportunities.

## PROMISING CHOICE: MAGNET SCHOOLS

Most readers have probably heard of the movie *Fame*, which told the story of a real-life performing arts school in New York. What fewer people may know is that *Fame* is actually a magnet school. About 4,000 of these magnets now operate across the country.[11] They are specialized schools that offer high-quality and unique programs, often in the arts or sciences, and give many students a chance to attend a public school other than the one to which they were assigned.

Magnets have been mainly the creation of federal judges who hoped to draw white children from the suburbs back into inner-city school districts. For the most part, magnet schools have been a great success. In many districts they are the only public schools competing with traditional schools for students.

So why can't every school be a magnet school? The main reason is that magnet schools are specifically set up and designed to avoid the normal rules, regulations, and bureaucracies of inner-city school systems. Federal judges simply don't have the time to run every school; if they did, most would be no better than what we have now.[12] A better idea is for parents to build on this model, wresting back control from the public school bureaucracy to create schools that they, and committed teachers, manage. This is the idea behind charter schools.

## PROMISING CHOICE: CHARTER SCHOOLS

In 1973 East Harlem District 4 ranked as the worst school district in New York City. But beginning in 1974, East Harlem Junior High teachers were given the flexibility to redesign their schools, and parents were allowed to choose the schools their children attended. Over the next fifteen years the district moved from last to 15th place among New York City's 32 districts.[13] East Harlem's example helped to launch the charter school movement in the United States.

The state that's shown the most ingenuity in this field is Arizona, with its network of 360 charter schools.[14] And Arizona is a case study of how charters can help get good teachers into the classroom and pay them more. Arizona's public schools offer a specific starting salary for every level of education. These salaries vary over a range of about $8,000, with any differences based entirely on years of teaching experience. In short, there's little flexibility and no way to reward the more successful teachers.

Charter schools, by contrast, are free to set their own salaries and reward teachers as they see fit. The result? Arizona's charter-school teachers earn more and the best teachers earn much more. Beginning teachers take home a paycheck that's an average of 6 percent more than in traditional public schools, and the salaries of new teachers can vary by as much as $21,000 depending on their expertise, experience, education, and other credentials (see figure 6.1).[15]

Washington, D.C., has also become a home to flourishing charter schools. And few school systems need charters more. The District of Columbia Public School System (DCPS) spends a whopping $14,000 per student on the average, enough to pay the tuition at some of our best private schools. Yet it is one of the most dysfunctional school systems

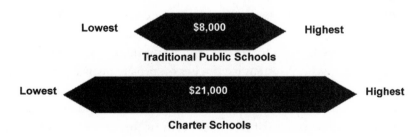

**FIGURE 6.1.** Salary Range Variance for Newly Hired Teachers in Arizona. (Source: Goldwater Institute survey. Reported in Lewis Solomon and Mary Gifford, "Teacher Accountability in Charter Schools," National Center for Policy Analysis, NCPA Brief Analysis No. 285, March 1, 1999)

in the country and consistently scores at the bottom on student achievement exams.

Faced with these miserable statistics, parents and teachers went looking for new options. Today, 15 percent of D.C. students—about 10,000 children—attend 33 charter schools.[16] Teachers have flocked to these new schools, drawn by the freedom to innovate and escape from the public system's stultifying bureaucracy. According to Paul Vance, school superintendent: "Teachers who have gone from our schools to the charter schools have found the freedom and collegiality which they were promised. . . . They saw an opportunity to do what they had dreamed of doing, to become unshackled."[17]

Vance's comments get to the heart of one of the bigger problems education faces today. Many good teachers burn out in public schools and drop out of teaching altogether. We may be able to coax that professional corps back into the classroom with the promise of higher salaries and more freedom to do their jobs. Charters are one positive step in that direction.

## PROMISING CHOICE: PRIVATE SCHOOLS

Why is it that parents are so attracted to private schools? The prestige? The chance to give kids a religious education? Greater safety? All of these may play a role in a parent's decision to go private. But the biggest reason, as a Brookings Institution study found, is simply that private schools do a better job than public schools.

And not just for the best students. Private schools have become a refuge for students who have difficulty navigating the public system. Not only do parents turn to private schools for help with difficult children, the public school system itself relies on private institutions to take the hardest cases. According to the U.S. Department of Education, public schools send more than 100,000 students to private schools. Students with serious emotional disturbances account for 40 percent of these students.[18]

Great as private schools are, parents who'd like to send their children face one big problem: they have to pay tuition in addition to all the taxes they already cough up for public schools. The good news is that this is starting to change, as more communities decide to devote a certain amount of public money for kids who go to private schools.

## Promising Choice: Vouchers

Milwaukee and Cleveland, for instance, offer "voucher" programs that allow inner-city, low-income students to attend private schools. Florida has a similarly innovative program, open to students who attend public schools that routinely fail to educate. And for more than a century, Maine and Vermont have paid private school tuition for students living in areas where there is no public school. Meanwhile, at least four states—Arizona, Illinois, Iowa, and Minnesota—let taxpayers take a tax deduction or tax credit for donations to organizations that provide private school scholarships to students.[19]

Critics of vouchers argue that using public money for private schools is wrong and at odds with other U.S. public policies.[20] In fact, allowing students to take public money to private schools is absolutely consistent with other government policies. The Medicare program funds health care for the elderly, but it doesn't tell seniors they can only enter government hospitals or see government doctors. Similarly, the GI Bill for returning World War II veterans and the modern Pell Grant program make tuition grants to students who attend private (even religious) colleges and universities as well as public institutions.

Most Americans believe the government has an obligation to see that every child has access to quality education. Yet just because government pays for something doesn't mean it also has to produce it. If government can't create and operate good schools in inner-city neighborhoods, parents should have the right to take their tax dollars elsewhere.

## Promising Choice: Homeschooling

In 2000, a precocious 12-year-old named George Abraham Thampy walked away with the prestigious National Spelling Bee trophy. His win helped to focus the nation's attention on a growing U.S. phenomenon. George, along with the second- and third-place winners, was homeschooled.

The number of children who sit down at their own kitchen table for their studies is rising by about 10 percent every year. Today, about two million of the nation's 47 million children get their education at home. Many parents see homeschooling as a smart economic decision. Instead of both parents heading off to work each day in order to pay for an expensive home in a good school district (and paying higher taxes in the process), homeschooling means a family can live anywhere. Moreover, these committed parents don't have to worry over whether their kids are getting a good education.

Homeschooling is now the choice of a wide spectrum of parents and not just, as the media often suggest, religious families. About the only thing all these parent-teachers have in common is a higher level of educational attainment.[21] And they are clearly able to deliver results. Homeschoolers as a whole do very well on standardized tests and compete for college scholarships. For instance, the winner of the National Geographic Bee in 2003 was a homeschooled 14-year-old from Washington state. In 2001, in fact, four of the top 10 finalists in the Geo Bee were educated at home.

## Lots of Money, No Results

For parents, the number one education concern is getting their children into good schools, and it's important that they have choices. But everyone else should be concerned that all our schools meet the test. Pulling mediocre and failing schools up to a level of excellence is a challenge. How can that challenge be met?

Perhaps the biggest roadblocks to reforming our schools are teachers unions, which unfortunately have come to see the school system as more of a jobs program than as a place where kids go to learn. To listen to the unions, schools only fail because they are starved for money and resources. Yet decades of academic research show there is simply no relationship between the amount of money that is spent and student achievement.[22]

We can even point to one notable experiment. What would happen if an unlimited amount of money were made available to bad schools? A federal judge in Kansas City, Missouri, decided to find out. He ordered Kansas City's school system to spend $2 billion of taxpayers' money. The system used this money to reduce the student-teacher ratio to 12 or 13 to one, to increase teacher pay, and to reduce teacher workloads. The schools installed television and animation studios as well as a robotics lab and financed field trips to Mexico and Senegal.

The result? Black student achievement scores did not improve at all, and the black-white achievement gap remained the same.[23] In all, it was an amazing failure. Academic studies suggest that Kansas City could have achieved more by simply giving bus fare to the kids and sending them to schools in the suburbs.[24] Instead, the judge spent $2 billion and achieved absolutely nothing.

## THE WILL TO COMPETE

The federal Department of Justice today employs hundreds of people whose only job is to investigate whether companies are "monopolies" and are therefore depriving consumers of choice and competition. Yet some of the biggest government-run programs—schools—continue to operate as total monopolies. Their customers, often low-income families, are held captive and unable to choose rival institutions. Like business monopolies, these schools have little incentive to improve their product.

Yet studies show that even the smallest amount of school choice will improve a school system. Harvard economist Caroline Hoxby has shown that when public and private schools compete for the same students, academic results improve. Among students transferring from public to private schools, Hoxby found a 12 percent increase in future wage gains and a 12 percent increase in the probability of college graduation. More interesting, Hoxby also found an eight-percentage point increase in the test scores of those students who remained in public schools.[25] By forcing public schools to compete in areas where they previously had a monopoly, school choice programs improved the educational outcomes of all students.

Wide anecdotal evidence also backs up Hoxby's conclusion. Giffen was perhaps the worst public elementary school in Albany, New York, when philanthropist Virginia Gilder offered private school scholarships to all of its students. Within months of the offer, the public school system responded with radical changes. The school board installed a new principal, hired two new assistant principals, moved 10 teachers to other schools, and set aside $125,000 for books, equipment, and teacher training.[26] Consider, too, that after Milwaukee's choice program was expanded to allow participation of up to 15 percent of public school enrollment, or about 15,000 students, the public school system closed its six worst schools and responded in other beneficial ways.[27]

## TEACHING THE TEACHERS

So if more money isn't the way to create a good school, what is? The most important key to effective learning is an effective teacher. Sadly, teacher preparation programs in this country remain stubbornly inadequate.

In 1983, the federal task force we mentioned, *A Nation at Risk*, found that half of newly employed mathematics, science, and English teachers weren't qualified to hold forth on those subjects. Two decades later, the Department of Education reported that only 41 percent of mathematics teachers had a major or minor in that subject, and too many science and English teachers also had no concentrated study in the areas they were teaching.[28] *A Nation at Risk* found that too many teachers were being drawn from the bottom quarter of graduating high school and college students. Twenty years later, a report found that college graduates with the lowest ACT and SAT scores were more likely to become teachers than those with the highest scores, despite the fact that teacher test scores are a good indicator of how well students will perform on achievement tests.[29]

Changing the culture of the teaching profession may be the greatest challenge we face in making all schools good schools. Teachers unions protect mediocre teachers and resist any system that would reward teachers based on their successes. They also control the school of education accrediting organization as well as the national professional standards board. The unions have successfully lobbied over a quarter of the states to shift the control of teacher licensing from state boards of education (which have lay members) to professional boards—again, controlled by unions. In sum, organized labor has total control over both the quality and supply of teachers.[30] It has become a formidable political force, the largest contributor to the Democratic Party in 2002.[31]

One of the greatest things about school choice is that it helps to force those schools that harbor the worst teachers to either change their ways or close down. School choice throws a market dynamic into public education, one that rewards success and punishes failure. With more competition, the best teachers would be promoted and the worst would likely leave the profession.[32]

Another way of ramping up the quality and supply of teachers is what's known as alternative certification. All but a handful of states now have ways for people with strong academic credentials to get into teaching, even if they haven't had the years of "education classes" unions tend to demand. These alternative routes attract people with specialized knowledge and life experience—physicists, writers, engineers—who then learn classroom management on the job.

New Jersey, for example, has had an alternative certification process in place since 1987, and today one in five of New Jersey's teachers enters the profession through this route every year. In Texas, 16 percent of new teachers are hired through the state's alternative process.[33] These successes aside, too many states still throw up needless barriers and burdensome regulations to alternative certification.

## WHAT CAN BE DONE?

Parents have largely been crowded out of the school system, and no longer have control over their children's education. They often have little or no information about the quality of the schools their children attend, and if some small snippet does appear it is usually too late to make a difference. Even when parents do have timely information, it can be an enormous struggle to transfer a child from a bad school to a better one. Those who consider sending their children to a private school are unlikely to get any financial help from the government. At a minimum, a reformed system should:

- Make it as easy as possible for parents to move their children into schools that are suited to meet their needs.
- Make it as easy as possible for parents and teachers to form new schools, outside the normal public school bureaucracy.
- Recognize the right of parents to remove their children from failing schools and place them in schools where they can succeed, even if that means that public school dollars end up paying private school tuition.
- Encourage programs that will attract talented people into the teaching profession.

# 7

~

# WOMEN AS SAVERS
# AND INVESTORS

KATHERINE, a 48-year-old mother of two, lives in the Washington, D.C., area and holds a government job. She's currently putting the maximum allowable amount every year into her work-sponsored retirement account, but she sometimes worries she waited too long before saving.

Katherine admits that in her earliest jobs she paid little attention to whether the companies offered retirement programs. She then went on to have her first child and took six years out of the workforce to stay at home with him and to have another. When she finally returned to the workforce as a lobbyist, her employer, a trade association, began making a small contribution every year into a defined-contribution retirement account for her. But by this point Katherine was newly divorced and "every dime of my own money was already accounted for. I wasn't able to contribute myself."

After three or four years at the trade association, Katherine did a three-month stint at a think tank. It wasn't long enough to collect any retirement money. From there she moved to a corporation in Texas. Katherine's mother had begun warning her that she should be thinking about the future, so Katherine started contributing money to the corporation-sponsored retirement account, and the company matched these funds. She also made an effort to put some money into an IRA for several years. Katherine then moved to a law firm but didn't stay long enough to meet the firm's vesting requirements. She took her government position a few years ago.

These days, Katherine contributes all she's allowed into her retirement fund, and the government matches 4 percent of her salary. Even so, she's worried it isn't enough. "The maximum I'm allowed to put in now is $13,000 a year, which isn't a whole lot when you are 48 years old and there isn't that much time left to contribute."

And Katherine is depending on that money. She believes she'll get something from Social Security but "I certainly wouldn't want to count on it." It also recently occurred to her that she could still be single when she retires. "It hit me that what I have is what I'll get in the end." She's also had some ups and downs with her retirement investments. She'd had her money in a stock portfolio, but in 1998 when the market tanked she transferred it to a lower-earning money-market fund. Only recently has she moved it back into a stock fund, with hope that it will grow faster. She still finds the 30-page monthly statement that "details all the buying and selling" confusing.

One thing that does cheer her is the thought that her home will one day prove a valuable retirement asset. It isn't paid off yet, but it has gone up in value considerably since she first purchased it. She estimates that it is probably worth about twice that of her own retirement savings of $130,000. "There is probably more possibility of growth in the house than what I can put into my own retirement account every year. That's what I'm counting on."

The roaring 1990s brought with it a lot of new questions about wealth and few have been probed more than the hot topic of "income inequality." Countless articles and studies have been devoted to the "gap" between the rich and poor. Some commentators say the gap doesn't matter, since everyone is better off than in the past. Others suggest a big difference in incomes is further proof that the American system is fundamentally unfair.

Yet despite all the attention, most commentators are missing the big income inequality story of our time. Careful studies have shown that the greatest income inequality is among senior citizens. The reason for this disparity is not differences in how much seniors earned before they retired but the degree to which they saved over their working lives.[1]

The Federal Reserve Bank conducts a "Survey of Consumer Finances" every three years, and its most recent retirement findings make for depressing reading.[2] Some 47 percent of all families with at least one worker between the ages of 21 and 64 have no retirement savings account. Of the nearly 48 million workers who do have an account, the median balance (half are larger, half are smaller) is only $27,000.

Workers nearing retirement are a little better off, though not by much.[3] About 30 percent of people between ages 55 and 64 have no retirement account, and among those who do the median balance is about $55,000. What sort of retirement will $55,000 buy you? A pension annuity of about $400 a month.

But women have an even harder time of it than men. One study found that among employees aged 18 to 62, women had only half as much on average in 401(k) and similar retirement accounts as men. And women nearing retirement age had an average balance of only 20 percent as much as their male counterparts (see figure 7.1).[4]

This might not be a disaster for women who have husbands with retirement income, but most find themselves alone in later years. Nearly half of all women today over age 65 are widows.[5] One-person households, as a rule, have smaller retirement savings and smaller Social Security benefits. Among men and women over the age of 65, those who are divorced are more likely to come in below the poverty line than those who are married. The chances of being poor are even higher for those who are widowed, separated, or who never married in the first place. Of all the seniors living in poverty, almost three-fourths are women (see figure 7.2).[6]

Why do women find it so difficult to save for their retirement? It's partly because our entire tax-advantaged retirement system is geared toward steady, full-time employees who work for firms with generous benefits. If you don't fall into that category—and many women don't—you are out of luck.

Women often choose jobs that allow them to look after their children. They periodically drop out of the workforce to take care of elderly family members. They work in industries that offer part-time hours,

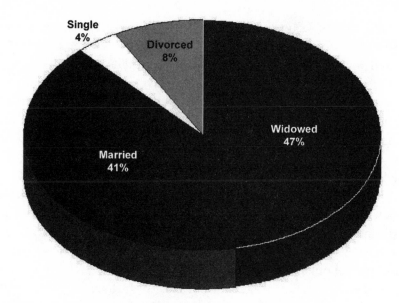

**FIGURE 7.1.** Marital Status of the Female Population Age 65 and Older, 2000. (Source: Congressional Budget Office)

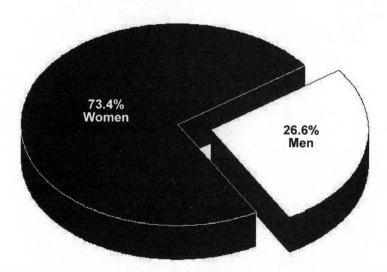

**FIGURE 7.2.** Percentage Distribution of Elderly Persons in Poverty. (Source: C. Eugene Steuerle, "Divorce and Social Security," National Center for Policy Analysis, NCPA Brief Analysis No. 291, May, 21, 1999)

thereby choosing flexibility over a higher salary or benefits. But exercising any of these options usually means that women write themselves out of the retirement system. Without a steady job, maintained over many years, most workers find it difficult if not impossible to save for their retirement future.

Take Susan, a 60-year-old living in California. Susan married young, and in the early years was the real breadwinner as her husband worked on his Ph.D. When they left California to go to his university in Boston, Susan withdrew what retirement savings she'd saved by working for a charity to finance the move. Five years later, when they moved to Washington, D.C., for Susan's career, she once again withdrew her retirement savings to get her family to their new home.

Close to 20 years after they married, Susan and her husband separated and ultimately divorced. Susan received half of her ex-husband's retirement savings. She admits that with the turmoil of her divorce, her usual financial discipline deteriorated and she didn't "look after" her half of the retirement money. She was also in Washington, moving from job to job, and at one point found herself out of work after a change in administration. Between funding employment gaps and her firm desire to pay for her daughter's college education, Susan burned through her portion of the retirement money.

In 1994, Susan went back to California and after a temporary assignment went to work for a county government. She left five years later and recently found out she'd built up $40,000 in retirement savings from her time on that job. Still, that's pretty much the extent of her retirement savings. She doesn't own any real estate, doesn't have a husband to provide a "safety net," and isn't counting on a lot from Social Security. Yet she also feels she made the right choices at the time: "We needed the money then. You think you'll earn forever, that things will take care of themselves," she says. "Now it's time to do some serious thinking."

## THE RETIREMENT TOOLBOX

All workers have available to them three basic tools for building up savings for a safe retirement: personal savings, Social Security, and employer-sponsored retirement plans. But women—because of their life choices and workforce behavior—find it harder to put these tools to work. Here's why:

## Personal Savings

Even the most disciplined person can find it a challenge to squirrel after-tax dollars away into a savings account. But for the many women who don't earn much, or for those who are homemakers and don't earn at all, it's more complicated. Even families with a comfortable income have to justify saving the money for retirement rather than setting it aside for preschool or college expenses, medical emergencies, or unplanned events in family life.

Workers who do manage to set money aside tend to find it's best to stash it in a tax-sheltered vehicle. Tax-advantaged savings can produce more than twice as much income as other taxable investments, depending on the tax bracket. An Individual Retirement Arrangement (IRA), for instance, is one of the best ways for workers who don't have access to an employer-sponsored retirement plan to save.

Unfortunately, the government puts arbitrary limits on these accounts that discourage people from saving more. Take the Spousal IRA, which allows the spouse of a wage earner to set aside up to $3,000 of pretax income, or $3,500 if the spouse is over age 50.[7] The sum grows tax-free until it is withdrawn during the retirement years.[8] This is exactly the sort of tool that would make a long-term retirement difference to married couples. Yet the $3,500 contribution limit is meager compared to what workers can contribute to employer-sponsored plans. There's also no reason why the limit shouldn't be higher. IRA deposits expand the nation's capital stock and thus our national income. The government usually gets a great deal of the money back as tax revenue. Several studies have even concluded that IRA tax incentives more than pay for themselves.[9]

Another smart personal savings device is that old American Dream of home ownership. When interest rates are low—as they have been recently—real estate becomes even more attractive. The federal government, too, encourages home buying through its policies. Under the current tax code, if a primary residence is sold for more than its cost basis, the sellers can usually pocket the profits from the sale tax-free. This has been a great incentive to many stay-at-home moms, whose avocation is increasing the value of their homes. They remodel, landscape, paint, and repair with the idea of collecting cash or trading up when they sell. Women like Katherine know it's a smart investment. Home equity is the principal asset of a large number of today's retirees.[10]

## Social Security

Many young workers have started to look at Social Security in a whole new light: They believe it will never be anything more than a supplement to their other retirement assets. As we shall see below, Social Security is already on the rocks, and everything suggests benefit cuts are likely in the future. Polls already show that many young people are more convinced they'll see a UFO than receive their Social Security benefits.[11]

Even if Social Security were able to keep all its promises, its payout is hardly enough to provide true financial independence in retirement. The average monthly Social Security benefit today is about $621 for women and $810 for men. By the time a 35-year-old accountant today earning about $30,000 a year retires, she'll take in $1,292 a month.[12] If she has no other assets, she'll have to survive on 50 percent of her former wages.

And that's assuming our accountant merrily works along exactly as she does now for the rest of her life. Chances are she won't. She could have interruptions in her employment. She might reduce her hours to accommodate family needs. Her Social Security benefit could then be significantly smaller than 50 percent of her working income. No wonder twice as many women as men retire in poverty.

## Employer-Sponsored Retirement Plans

Have you ever stopped to wonder why companies go through the hassle of providing their employees with benefits rather than just paying them more in wages? Employer benefits are, after all, an expense just like wages. If Congress passed a law tomorrow making benefits illegal, companies would tend to increase employee wages by about the same amount that they now spend on benefits.

The answer is tax law. Employers can provide employees with a much better deal on benefits than workers can obtain themselves. When it comes to retirement savings in particular, there are huge differences between what people at a workplace can obtain in tax-free savings and what they can save tax-free on their own. Employer-sponsored retirement plans have therefore become a valued part of employee compensation. They've also undergone dramatic changes since the days when they were first offered.

## Defined-Benefit Plans

With the end of World War II came the beginning of the primary type of employer retirement program, known as a *defined-benefit plan*. Employees acquired pension benefits based on their wages and years of service to the company. Companies promised a specific annual retirement sum, which was often payable for the entirety of a worker's retirement years. The typical "company man" who worked for the same employer his entire life could expect a pension benefit that was 60 to 70 percent of his final paycheck. Millions of employees are still participating in such defined-benefit plans today, even though most companies no longer establish them. They've fallen out of favor because of four big problems.

First, although the plans work well for people who loyally serve the same firm from the first day to the last day of their employment, they can be a huge disappointment for the increasing number of workers who switch jobs. Most defined-benefit plans calculate their pension payouts under formulas that are "back-end loaded" in terms of workers' pay. Companies weigh a worker's 40th year of service much more highly than, say, the 10th year of service.

Consider a woman who works for four different companies—each for 10 years—that all have identical pension plans. When she slips into retirement, she will get four separate pension checks. But her combined income will still be less than half of what it would have been if she had stuck with one company the full 40 years.

So employees who switch companies usually end up sacrificing big pension benefits, even though they may have been busily employed their whole career. The system penalizes women in particular, since many of them go in and out of the workforce to have children or run homes. But it is no friendlier to men who want to take advantage of new work opportunities. Companies are realizing that the days of one-company employees are fading and that they need to change their pension plans to reflect this more dynamic labor market.

Second, for most of the period in which companies offered defined-benefit plans they weren't required to "fund" them. Firms were able to promise benefits without adequately saving and investing to be able to keep these promises. If the employer went broke, employees could lose some or all of their benefits. When Studebaker filed for bankruptcy in 1963, autoworkers received only 15 percent of the pension benefits they had been promised.[13]

Third, federal legislation made defined-benefit plans unattractive to the companies that offered them. When employers first started to default on their pension obligations, Congress passed legislation requiring them to begin funding their defined-benefit plans.[14] This legislation also created the Pension Benefit Guaranty Corporation (PBGC) to provide default insurance for private pension plans.

But this insurance doesn't work like other insurance. Although companies with defined-benefit pension plans are required to pay premiums to the PBGC, the premiums charged do not reflect real risks. Fully funded company plans that are at little risk of default pay premiums that are way above the value of the insurance to the firm. But plans that are at a high risk of default don't pay anywhere near the sort of premiums their risk warrants. The PBGC socializes the risk of pension default by overcharging healthy plans and undercharging sick ones.[15]

Young companies establishing new pension plans, therefore, have every incentive to avoid the PBGC and its big levies. The one bit of good news that emerges from all of this is that in its attempt to regulate and reform the private pension system, Congress gave companies a way out.[16] It allowed the creation of *defined-contribution* plans (which we'll address below), including the famous 401(k) plan.[17]

The final problem with defined-benefit plans is that it has become increasingly expensive to honor the promises these plans have made. The programs were based on actuarial assumptions that no longer hold true. Retirees are living far longer than they did 60 years ago, when many of the plans were established. In order for companies to fund their plans, employees have to be willing to accept less in wages (so that more can go to the pension fund) or they have to be willing to accept lower monthly benefits during retirement. (If you think this all sounds eerily like the problems facing Social Security, you're partly right.)

Moreover, not all employees are the same. They have different needs and different attitudes toward risk. So instead of continuing with a one-size-fits-all approach that is guaranteed to make at least part of the workforce unhappy, employers searched for a system in which employees could make more of their own choices. Companies have found it is possible (for the same amount of dollars) to create a pension system in which workers call the shots. It's known as a defined-contribution plan.

## Defined-Contribution Plans

The most important difference between a defined-benefit and a defined-contribution plan is that the latter offers no specific payout at the time of retirement. The employee "owns" the account and is entitled to however much it accumulates.[18] Employees designate a certain portion of their salary to go into the plan each year, and companies usually match this amount.

A typical plan, for instance, would encourage the employee to contribute 4 percent of her gross compensation (before taxes) to the plan. The company would then match those contributions dollar for dollar. Employees are governed by federal law as to how much they are able to set aside before taxes. In 2003, the amount was $12,000.[19]

But that's only the start of the differences between the old and new plans. Another change is that employees are in charge of making their own investment choices in 401(k) plans, though companies usually limit the range of options. Also, so long as the employees are fully "vested," they do not lose the employer match if they move to another company. The amount of money they build up stays in the account even when they change jobs. Today, more than half of all workers with employer-provided retirement plans are in these much more mobile and flexible defined-contribution plans.[20]

Defined-contribution plans marked a defining change in the way companies and employees viewed retirement benefits. There used to be a day when companies expected an employee to provide lifelong service, and a worker in return expected the firm to look after her in old age. That's no longer the case. Workers now expect the right to trade up to better jobs with different employers. Companies want the freedom to hunt for better employees. The best way to accommodate this new workplace dynamic is for companies to reward their workers with retirement funds while they are employed but then allow employees to take those accounts with them when they leave.

The only catch is that the worker must have the sense about her to competently manage her own investments. In return for flexibility and freedom in the workforce, she has assumed the risks for her own retirement future.

## RISK?

What are your own retirement goals? For most Americans, future dreams of retirement are fairly modest. We want to know that we can retire with some level of comfort—take the occasional trip, play the occasional round of golf, buy our grandchildren birthday presents. We also don't want to worry we'll run out of money before we die. What retirement plan is more likely to give us that comfort and security? The answer isn't what you might think.

At first glance, you might assume that a defined-benefit plan is far less risky. Workers don't have to worry about making bad investment decisions over their lives. And since defined-benefit plans usually pay out through all your retirement years, you don't have to worry about running out of money.

But, there are downsides. As we have seen, you are likely to lose much of your defined-benefit pension if you switch jobs during your career. It is also usually impossible to pass along anything you built up after you die. Companies typically stop paying once the retiree passes away. Defined-contribution plans don't have these problems. Aside from certain vesting requirements (which we'll discuss below), 401(k) owners can take all their money with them when they switch jobs. They can also pass what is left of these retirement savings to heirs when they die.

Richard Hinz, director of pensions research at the U.S. Department of Labor, conducted a simulation of 100,000 representative American workers. His conclusion? Take into account all factors, and defined-contribution plans are actually less risky than defined-benefit pensions. A plan that bases benefits on tenure and salary is unlikely to keep pace with a portable investment account, especially given the likelihood workers will leave their company or that their salary may flatten out before the end of their career.[21]

Women, as it happens, already are bigger consumers of defined-contribution plans. Many of the companies with defined-benefit plans are traditionally unionized, male-dominated industries—in steel or in autoworking, for instance. Among women with an employer-provided retirement plan, enrollment in defined-contribution plans is twice that of defined-benefit plans.[22]

Clearly, defined-contribution plans have their advantages and are the way of the future. Yet while they've solved many of the drawbacks of the old system, they have their own hitches. The following are a few examples.

## PROBLEM NO. 1:
### VEXING VESTING

Companies may be reconciled to the fact that they won't keep employees for life, but most believe workers should have to put in a certain amount of time before they receive benefits. Many companies therefore have vesting requirements, which require workers to tally up a certain number of years before they get the key to their full promised retirement benefits.

Employees who plunk money into a defined-contribution plan are entitled to what they've contributed. But they usually aren't given access to a company's full matching contribution until they've logged a certain amount of time. Those vesting requirements used to top 10 or 15 years. Today, by law, companies must fully vest their employees after six years. But even a six-year requirement is a challenge for those women who go in and out of the workforce.[23] So why have vesting at all?

Some employers argue that vesting allows them to recover some of the administrative costs of workers who pop in and out of their jobs. But these costs can't be that much of a burden, given that many employers competing for highly skilled workers have already dropped vesting requirements and match employees' contributions from their first day on the job.

It's more likely that companies view vesting requirements as a way to keep people on the job. Firms use long vesting requirements to reward employees who stay with the firm and to punish those who leave to work for a rival.

There's nothing wrong in principle with companies rewarding longevity, especially if it's a compensation bargain both sides agree to in a free market. But retirement plans involve something more than the voluntary exchange of work for pay and benefits. It is taxpayers, after all, who underwrite the ability of companies to offer tax-free savings to workers. There is a social purpose to that subsidy, that of encouraging people to accumulate assets to fund living expenses during the years of their retirement.

Employers who demand onerous vesting requirements are using tax-subsidized vehicles to achieve their private, corporate ends. Vesting requirements not only undermine the social goal of encouraging people to save for their retirements, they interfere with labor market mobility.

## Problem No. 2:
### Confining Contributions

For a country founded on equality, one of the more remarkable aspects of today's retirement system is the different and arbitrary limits on how much people can put into tax-deferred savings (see figure 7.3). Some people are able to deposit as much as $40,000 per year in tax-deferred savings plans.[24] Others are hit with the $12,000 maximum in allowed contributions to a 401(k) plan.[25] Those who don't have an employer-sponsored plan, including those who don't work, are limited to a $3,500 maximum contribution to an IRA account.[26]

These bizarre limits make it that much harder for women like Katherine to save for the future. Women are more likely to work in an industry that doesn't offer an employer-provided retirement plan. Even

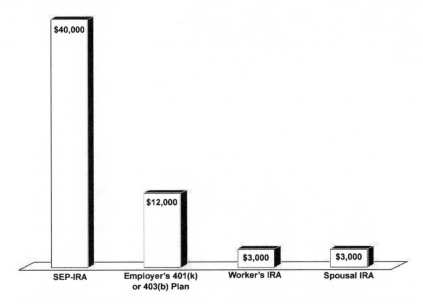

**FIGURE 7.3.** Limits on Contributions to Tax-Favored Savings Plans in 2003 (for individuals under age 50; persons age 50 and above are allowed additional, catch-up contributions, and couples with incomes above $70,000 could not deduct IRA contributions from their income taxes).

if their company does provide retirement help, women are less likely to qualify because they are part-time or temporary workers. And women are more likely to move in and out of the labor market.[27]

Even taking a small break from work can have a large impact on retirement benefits. Consider a woman who quits work from the age of 25 to 30 to have children. If she returns to the workforce and labors away until retirement, she will find that her 401(k) accumulation when she retires is 20 to 30 percent smaller because of that five-year gap.[28] And during her absence, the government will also limit the amount of money she can put into tax-deferred savings such as a spousal IRA.

If we as a society have decided it is desirable to encourage people to save for their own retirement, the limits on saving should not be arbitrary. It's hard to come up with a socially justifiable reason why the amount a person is allowed to save tax-free should rest on where she works, or even whether she is in the labor market.

## PROBLEM NO. 3:
## INVESTMENT 101

One big difference between defined-benefit and defined-contribution plans is that workers in the latter are allowed to make their own investment choices. Some employees cherish this freedom. Others fear it and view it as a burden. The fear is not unwarranted. Employees nationwide have done a poor job of investing their own money.

When Watson Wyatt did a study of 503 employers from 1990 through 1995, it found that defined-benefit plans average an annual rate of return that was 1.9 percentage points better than 401(k) plans—10 percent versus 8.1 percent.[29] That's a big difference. If you were to invest $4,000 a year for 30 years, at 10 percent the account will grow to about $690,880, while at 8.1 percent it will grow to only $480,224. That's a gap of $210,656 and a much less enjoyable retirement.[30]

It might be reasonable to expect that better-educated, more sophisticated employees do a better job of investing their money. Not so. A study by the National Center for Policy Analysis looked at the 401(k) performance of employees who worked for firms that specialize in investing other people's money and giving advice on how money should be invested. The conclusion: Over a four-year period ending in 1998, none of the financial service firms' average 401(k) earnings came close to matching the performance of the stock market as a whole or a mixed portfolio of stocks and bonds.[31]

So why do workers make such a hash of their 401(k) plans? It is usually because they make one or both of two bad investment decisions. They either invest in what they know (their own employer's stock) or they invest in what is "safe" (money-market funds and bonds).

The most glaring example of the first mistake is Enron employees who invested heavily in their own company. Employees watched the energy firm's stock get roiled by scandal and had to stand by as their retirement funds disappeared into the ether. A recent survey of 105 larger public companies found 40 in which workers had invested more than half their 401(k) assets in their own company's stock.[32] Workers tend to think they have an inside track at their companies, but no matter how much information or confidence an investor has it is always risky to put all the financial eggs into one basket.

Then there are those employees who choose to put their money in "safe" securities, even though these vehicles pay low rates of return. Lower-paid employees in particular tend to take this conservative route. Take a look at figure 7.4, which shows the 401(k) choices of the employees at a private company, grouped by incomes. The lowest-paid employees invested almost two-thirds of their assets in a money market fund or a bond fund. The highest paid employees invested some 85 percent of their assets in stocks.[33]

Now compare the two portfolios. If history is any guide, the all-stock portfolio will rack up 10 times as much wealth as the all-bond portfolio over the course of a work life.[34] Lower-income workers might feel more at

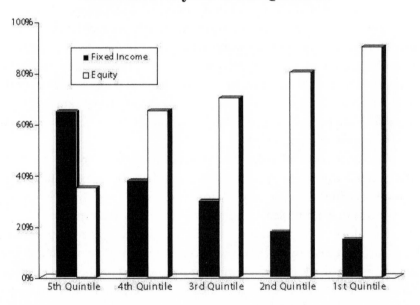

## Sample 401(k) Plan: Asset Allocation by Income Quintile

**FIGURE 7.4.** Sample 401(k) Plan: Asset Allocation by Income Quintile. (Source: Brooks Hamilton and Scott Burns, "Reinventing Retirement Income," National Center for Policy Analysis, NCPA Policy Report No. 248, December 2001, Figure III, p. 13)

ease with less risk, but when all is said and done they'll end up with far less for their retirement than if they'd invested their money more aggressively.

Most readers won't be surprised to learn that men and women invest in different ways. Studies show that women, like low-income workers, are more risk averse. They, for instance, choose bonds over stocks.[35] Then again, men are more likely than women to keep changing their portfolios. That sort of excessive trading reduces the net returns on men's investments by a full percentage point relative to women.[36] It turns out that men are a little *too* confident in their own abilities, according to psychological studies. As one economist put it: "Men tend to think their successes are the result of their own skill rather than dumb luck."[37]

## PROBLEM NO. 4:
## ADVICE IS NOT ADVISED

As unfortunate as some of these investing errors may be, at least these workers are making their own investment choices. Many others do not. At least one-third of the lowest-paid employees fail to select a 401(k) portfolio. As a result, their funds are invested in a default option that their employer has chosen for them. And for most companies, the default option is a low-earning money-market fund.[38]

Why don't employers automatically route their employees' retirement money into portfolios that make more sense? The simple answer: lawsuits. The corporate world is paralyzed with fear that their employees will later sue them if they make riskier investments that go sour in a bear market. This anxiety is also the reason why companies refuse to give their employees investment advice.[39]

Yet even the tiniest bit of guidance from an employer would go a long way. Mountains of economic research already point to a simple conclusion: The best and most prudent strategy for the nonprofessional investor is to put her money into the market as a whole. One efficient way of doing this is to invest in an "index fund."

The idea of an index fund is that it holds stocks that are representative of the entire market. History shows that the market as a whole tends to outperform professional mutual fund managers. Take the 15-year period ending on December 31, 2001. An investment in the Vanguard

500 Index 15 years ago would have averaged an annual rate of return of 13.56 percent. That's a far sight better than the average mutual fund return and is almost a point and a half better than the average equity fund return. Financial columnist Scott Burns calls this the "couch potato" approach to investing, and he notes that couch potatoes consistently tuck away a lot more money than they would if they'd handed their money to a professional stock-picker.[40]

The point here is that it's very hard to beat the market, and even an unsophisticated investor who is willing to ride the general market's ups and downs will do well over time. What we need is a simple change in the law that would allow companies to direct more of their employees' money into higher-performance retirement funds like these. The change would need to provide employers with protection from lawsuits if they were to default employees into index funds or similarly broad-based portfolios or if they were to encourage their workers to make those investment choices.[41] The result would be safer and more lucrative retirements for millions of Americans.

## PROBLEM NO. 5:
### TAKING A SECOND LOOK AT TAX DEFERRAL

Urging people to invest and save is obviously a good thing, and Congress should be doing more in that regard. But investors should also be aware that money saved for the future can be subject to certain penalties.[42] Until our lawmakers solve *that* problem, many senior citizens are looking at a less comfortable retirement than they might have expected.

As is so often the case, the source of the problem is the tax law. Most people believe (and they are reinforced in this belief by financial advisers) that by putting money into 401(k)s, IRAs, and other accounts they'll be reducing their lifetime taxes. Workers have come to this conclusion for two reasons. First, they view tax deferral as an interest-free loan. The ability to invest pretax dollars means that taxpayers get to earn a return on the government's money. They can use the funds today and pay the government its due much later in life. Second, most workers expect they'll be in a lower tax bracket after they retire, since their incomes will be lower. Tax deferral in retirement accounts means shifting tax paying from a time when you are in a higher bracket to a time when you are in a lower one.

This second idea sounds good, but it's wrong—and especially for low- and moderate-income families. The reason is the Social Security benefits tax. Officially, this is a tax on Social Security benefits, but in practice it is a tax on other retirement income. The more a worker saves over her life, the greater Social Security benefits tax she'll pay when she withdraws that private retirement money. Today, only about one-fifth of seniors pay the benefits tax. But the level at which the tax kicks in is not indexed for inflation, and so by the time today's young people hit their retirement years they'll all be paying the penalty.[43] (For more on the benefits tax, see chapter 9 on retirees.)

Most people in their twenties today who earn less than $100,000 a year will face a higher tax bracket when they retire. What they are really doing is deferring their retirement tax payments from a time in their life when they are in a lower tax bracket to a time when they are in a higher one. Those stifling higher rates can more than wipe out the good effects of having an interest-free loan from the government over the years.

That's the bad news. The good news is that researchers have found that workers almost always come out ahead if they invest through a Roth IRA.[44] Like a regular IRA, Roth IRAs allow tax-free growth. But deposits to a Roth IRA are made with after-tax dollars and withdrawals are tax-free. People can therefore pay their taxes at a time in their lives when they are in a more affordable tax bracket.

## THE BUSH TAX CUT

President George W. Bush's 2001 tax cut addresses a number of these problems, though only for a small amount of time. The law will raise the amount that people can contribute to IRAs and Roth IRAs from $2,000 to $5,000 per person by 2008. This in itself is a major step toward narrowing the arbitrary difference between contribution limits for people who have company-sponsored 401(k)s and for those who save in independent accounts. Moreover, the act also allows employers to begin offering a 401(k) plan that is taxed like a Roth IRA (with after-tax dollars) in 2006.

But Congress, worried about the "cost" of these programs, included a trip wire. These good provisions will all disappear and we'll revert to the old tax rules after 2010. At that point, we'll be no better off than we were in 2001.

## WHAT CAN BE DONE?

Our retirement system is in desperate need of reform. Americans need more encouragement to save, and they also have to be certain that the rules aren't going to change every couple of years. Everyone would benefit from a smarter, forward-looking retirement system. But reform would also need special benefits for women, who fulfill different roles in our economy:

- Accumulating retirement assets is more important to women because they live longer and are more likely to be alone in their retirement years.
- Women are more adversely affected by long vesting periods because they switch jobs more frequently.
- Women are hit harder by the practice of denying employer-provided benefits to part-time workers because they are the workers who usually fill these shorter-time jobs.
- Women struggle more with arbitrary limits on retirement savings contributions because they are more likely to have an IRA as their only tax-advantaged saving option.
- Women are hurt more by a system that discourages employers from providing sound investment advice because they are more likely to need and take that advice.
- Finally, women suffer from a lack of access to the Roth method of taxation because they are more likely to have low and moderate incomes.

We've run through some of the specifics of reform in this chapter. But far more important than the details is a commitment to a bold, new retirement system. That system needs to:

- create retirement plans that are personal and portable, which workers can take with them from job to job;
- eliminate rules that arbitrarily punish people who work part-time, or switch jobs frequently, or move in and out of the labor market;
- get rid of arbitrary ceilings on retirement savings plan contributions that unfairly favor one industry over another;
- establish ways to encourage people to invest wisely and prudently over the course of their careers; and
- set up a tax system that doesn't unfairly penalize people because of changes in their tax bracket over time.

Some of the reforms contained in the Bush tax cut of 2001 are a step in the right direction. But these are temporary, and much work remains.

# WOMEN AND
# SOCIAL SECURITY

ANNA JANIS, an 80-year-old living in Louisville, Colorado, is a woman who has done a fair amount in her time. As a young lady from a poor family, she worked part-time to put herself through college. For the next 18 years she looked after a family home, a husband, and two children. Then in 1974, having brushed up on her credentials, she threw herself back into the workforce to compete with far younger college graduates. She labored as a substitute teacher, as director of a business school, and finally as an industrial recruiter. Over all those years she dutifully paid the mandatory portion of her paycheck into the Social Security system.

Her career unfortunately came to an end in 1986 when Anna's husband, George, developed leukemia and she retired to look after him. Because she'd spent most of her life at home as a mother or moving upward through different jobs, she hadn't been at any one place long enough to qualify for a pension. That left her for the next five years collecting some of the Social Security she'd contributed.

From the start, Anna didn't receive what was technically owed her. She'd taken early retirement at the age of 63, but she still had some part-time income. So she had to forfeit $1 of her Social Security benefits for every $2 of extra earnings.[1] Yet even that small amount was more than she'd later receive. When George died in 1991, Anna discovered she had to make a choice. She could either continue to collect the Social Security that she'd paid in over the years, or she could claim a "survivor" benefit from her husband's Social Security. Since the survivor's benefit was twice her own, Anna opted to receive the larger check. But in doing so she had to forfeit the benefit based on her own contributions to Social Security during her own career. "I paid in all those years, but it had no value in the end," she says. "I'd thrown in so much, with nothing to show for it."

Most conversations about Social Security focus on how we might fundamentally alter the program for the future. Should we nudge up the retirement age? Must we cut benefits? Should the younger generation be allowed private accounts? (We will touch on some of these questions later in the book.) What aren't as well discussed are terrible inequities in the current Social Security program—inequities that have been there for years. These defects hamstring the lives of millions of seniors on a daily basis and no one more than women.

Like the tax system, Social Security was designed for the traditional married couple with a husband in the workforce and a wife at home. As such, the system has special provisions to ensure that stay-at-home women are able to claim retirement benefits. After a husband finally retirees, his wife is entitled to a monthly spousal benefit that is equal to 50 percent of her husband's benefit. After her husband's death, the spousal benefit ends. But at that point a wife is entitled a survivor's benefit equal to the entire amount of her husband's benefit. Considering that only one person has worked and paid taxes throughout a couple's lifetime, the traditional family has a relatively good Social Security deal.

This set-up also means women have a much bigger stake in the structure of the Social Security program. Granted, if a wife works full-time and the husband stays home, Social Security will pay a spousal benefit to her husband after she retires. But as it happens, fewer than 2 percent of retirees who claim the spousal benefit are men.[2] Moreover, women rely to a much greater degree on Social Security checks in the long term. The average life expectancy at birth for a woman is still 5.7 years longer than

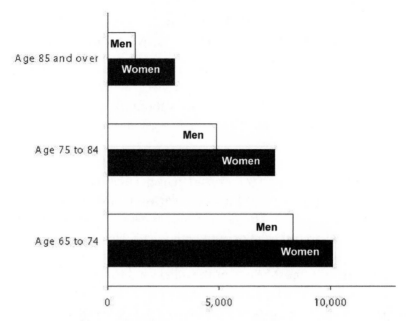

**FIGURE 8.1.** Elderly Population (year 2000, in millions). (Source: Census 2000 Brief: The 65 Years and Over Population: 2000, October 2001, Figure 2. http://www.census.gov/prod/2001pubs/c2kbr01-10.pdf)

for a male. And the older the beneficiary, the more likely that person is to be female (see figure 8.1).[3]

Despite all this, the millions of women dependent on our federal retirement system are still stuck navigating a Byzantine system of rules that govern everything from marriage and divorce to the decision to have a career in the first place. Wives working alongside their husbands ultimately must, like Anna Janis, choose between claiming their own benefits or what might be a much larger spousal benefit. Growing numbers of divorced women are unable to claim any of their husband's retirement funds. Widows must choose between staying home and collecting Social Security or sometimes sacrificing benefits if they work. The system is a lottery in which every woman pulls a ticket and then waits through life's twists and turns to discover whether she'll retire comfortably or be left scraping to make ends meet.

## Problem No. 1:
## A Penny Saved Is a Penny Gone

Over the years, more and more workers have watched their Social Security taxes disappear out of their paychecks with growing unease. Younger workers in particular read stories about the dire state of Social Security finances and wonder if they'll ever get anything back from the money they are paying in.

A significant number of American retirees have already been forced to kiss goodbye to the money they paid in over a lifetime. Who are these people? Working spouses, and in particular women who earned wages and paid taxes. As Anna Janis's story shows, working women face an unsavory Social Security choice upon retirement. They may either claim Social Security benefits in their own right or claim their husband's spousal benefits. It must be one or the other—no ifs, ands, or buts.

Viewed from any angle, there's nothing here that looks fair. On the one hand, women who choose to collect their own Social Security find that they usually receive only slightly more than a woman who never worked a day in her life but receives a spousal benefit. On the other hand, women who agree to take their husband's (usually larger) spousal benefit must agree to give up all the payroll taxes they paid in over many years of toil.

Consider how this Catch-22 affects couples that stay married right on through their retirement years. A 25-year-old wife with a high school education will increase the lifetime Social Security taxes she and her husband will pay by 74 percent but will increase its benefits by only 17 percent if she goes to work full-time (see figure 8.2). For college graduates, a woman's decision to work will increase family taxes by 88 percent, but benefits will go up a measly 24 percent (see figure 8.3).[4]

In this way, Social Security imposes a big penalty on two-earner couples.[5] Spouses with high school educations in the labor market will give Social Security some $40,000 over and above any extra benefits they receive (in today's dollars). Likewise, married college graduates will hand over some $80,000 more than they'll ever get back. There is very little upside under Social Security when both husband and wife hold jobs.

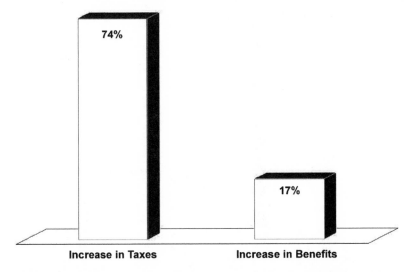

**74%**

**17%**

**Increase in Taxes**                    **Increase in Benefits**

**FIGURE 8.2.** Changes in Social Security Costs and Benefits When a Nonworking Spouse Enters the Labor Market: High School Graduates. Assumptions: The couple is 25 years of age and both spouses earn the average wage paid to high school graduates over their work lives. (Source: Calculations by Andy Rettenmaier, Private Enterprise Research Center, Texas A&M University)

## Problem No. 2:
## Breaking Up Is Hard to Do

When Social Security first opened for business, few people in the country considered divorce an option—no matter how messy or unhappy the relationship. The designers of the program focused instead on a different worry: that some women would try to marry older single men for the sole purpose of scooping up their retirement benefits once they joined the dearly departed. The minutes from the Federal Advisory Council that formulated the 1939 amendments for the original Social Security benefits therefore set a minimum marriage time limit as a "defense against a designing woman."[6]

Social Security to this day still enforces the rule that only a person who is married for 10 years is entitled to full benefits based on a spouse's contribution. Of all the problems with that cut-off, the most obvious is

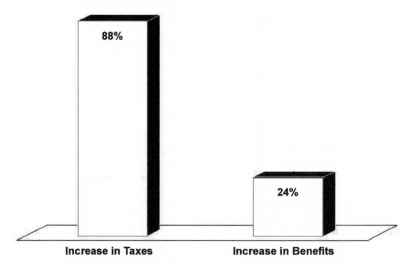

FIGURE 8.3. Changes in Social Security Costs and Benefits When a Nonworking Spouse Enters the Labor Market: College Graduates. Assumptions: The couple is 25 years of age and both spouses earn the average wage paid to college graduates over their work lives. (Source: Calculations by Andy Rettenmaier, Private Enterprise Research Center, Texas A&M University)

its arbitrariness. The woman who toughs it through nine years and 363 days of a marriage is no more entitled to her husband's spousal benefit than one who is married for a single week.

But the bigger problem is that the 10-year rule is completely out of sync with our modern era of failed marriages. The unfortunate reality is that 50 percent of first marriages and 60 percent of subsequent marriages in the United States now end in divorce.[7] Moreover, the average marriage that ends in divorce lasts only seven years.[8]

Because the private pension industry has similar rules, a significant number of divorced seniors have far less income in their retirement years than they might have expected.[9] The situation is particularly dire for the many women who marry and stay at home to look after a family, only to find themselves in a divorce before the 10-year limit. These women are left with no claim to Social Security despite the years they spent "working" in the family home.

## PROBLEM NO. 3:
## THE BLACK-BALLED WIDOW

Of all the things Social Security has come to stand for in the United States, it has a special reputation as a provider for widows and children. The payout, while not luxurious, is substantive. A mother with two children, for instance, can count on a monthly benefit check equal to about 60 percent of her late husband's income, and this benefit continues until her children reach age 16.[10] Children, too, receive benefit checks that continue until they are 18 years old.[11]

That's the upside. The downside is that Social Security also requires widows to adhere to strict rules that can make life difficult. Unlike private sector programs, Social Security survivor benefits are premised on the idea that a surviving spouse will stay at home with the children while the benefits are received. Any woman who works while also claiming Social Security benefits gets hit with a huge "earnings" penalty—which is usually big enough to discourage any work at all.

How bad is it? Consider a fictional Diane, a young wife and mother whose husband is killed in a work-site accident. If Diane goes to work, she will lose $1 in benefits for every $2 of money she makes above $11,520 (the 2003 threshold). This in itself is close to a 50 percent tax on her labor market income.

If Diane were then to add in a 15 percent income tax, a 15.3 percent Social Security tax, and a 7 percent state and local income tax, her total marginal tax rate would be 87 percent—meaning she would keep less than 13 cents of each additional dollar she earns. If Diane were to find a good job, pushing her into the 28 percent income tax bracket, her marginal tax rate would be 100 percent. The government would be taking every last penny of each additional dollar she earned.

Unsurprisingly, many women find it more financially advantageous to stay at home. But for widows like Diane this can cause long-term financial stress. The federal money flows in the early years; but once her youngest child hits age 16, Diane will be completely cut off from benefits until she is old enough to qualify for her own Social Security retirement. So Diane faces a choice. She can stay at home, never acquiring the job skills she will need to sustain her through the 25 or so years between when her benefits are cut off and when she qualifies for retirement. Or she can go to work to prepare for her future and have the government sock her with some of the highest marginal rates found anywhere in our economy.

## PROBLEM NO. 4: ROLLING THE DICE

Altogether, Social Security rules for work, spousal and survivor benefits, and divorce add up to a system that is arbitrary and unfair. Consider some of the following circumstances, all of which are particularly frustrating for women:[12]

- The wife who is the head of a household of several children and works 40 years at $10,000 a year will pull in a substantially lower Social Security check than a woman who never worked and never raised children but was married to a wealthy worker for 10 years and one day.
- A couple with $50,000 in combined annual income that is split between a husband who earned $45,000 and a wife who earned $5,000 will receive substantially more in Social Security benefits than a couple who each earned $25,000 a year.
- A woman who is married for 10 years and one day is entitled to full spousal benefits. If she is married for 10 years minus one day, she is entitled to nothing. But if a man has five wives in succession—each a marriage lasting 10 years—each of his wives qualifies for the spousal benefit, and they are collectively entitled to hundreds of thousands of dollars more in Social Security benefits than the woman who was married her entire lifetime to one spouse who pays the same amount in taxes.
- A divorced woman who later marries a much older man will get substantially more benefits on the average than a divorced woman who later marries a worker of her same age. That's because women who marry older workers are more likely to get survivor's benefits, which are far more generous than spousal benefits.

## What Can Be Done?

As we read a few chapters ago, the problem with the income tax system is that it refuses to treat couples as individuals. Social Security's problem is exactly opposite: it refuses to treat couples as couples, each with a one-half stake in taxes and benefits.[13]

One popular fix is something known as earnings sharing.[14] Under this plan, Social Security taxes would be divided at the time they were paid. Half would go to the husband and half to the wife. Think of it as similar to the way property is divided in community property states.

If the Social Security program had adopted earnings sharing from the beginning, the scenarios we cited above would never happen. Consider the two couples that each earned $50,000. Under earnings sharing, half of the husband's $45,000 in payroll taxes would go to his wife, and half of her $5,000 in payroll taxes would go to him. Likewise, the husband and wife who each earned $25,000 would split their payroll taxes. Couples with the same income would receive the same benefits, regardless of how the income was originally generated.

Earnings sharing would also solve the divorce problem, since it would only last for as long as a couple was married. Women who stayed at home to raise a family would still rack up Social Security benefits even if their marriages didn't make it to the 10-year deadline. Men (or women) would not be able to create additional benefits under the system by engaging in serial 10-year marriages.

That isn't to say that earnings sharing is picture perfect. For instance, if Social Security had adopted it from the beginning, many retired widows who never worked would be receiving less in benefits than they do today. Why? Because a widow would probably get more from a benefit payment equal to 100 percent of her dead husband's benefit (as she gets now) than she would a benefit based on half of his contribution. However, this is likely to be less of a problem in the future because so many women are choosing to enter the workforce.

Earnings sharing faces another problem: record keeping. If we today tried to go back and divide earnings between husbands and wives, the Social Security Administration would face the daunting task of figuring out who was married to whom and for how long—for every worker in

America. (In the current system, marriage only needs to be verified at the time benefits are paid.) Considering how the Social Security Administration already struggles to keep up with its paperwork, this sounds like a recipe for bureaucratic disaster.

Earnings sharing is a better solution when integrated with some of the other reform proposals being discussed in Congress. One frequently discussed reform is the creation of individual retirement accounts. Since earnings sharing would only apply to the new accounts, we could avoid the record-keeping problem of trying to reconstruct the past.

Scholars from the National Center for Policy Analysis have suggested some specifics for such a reform.[15] They advocate that deposits to individual retirement accounts be divided equally between husband and wife at the time deposits are made. At the time benefits were realized, however, there would be a government-backed guarantee that no one would be worse off under the new system than they would be under the old one.

We will discuss the idea of individual retirement accounts in future chapters. Such a system—in addition to curing the unfairness and arbitrariness that plague today's system—would also help ensure that all workers (especially women) have safer and more comfortable retirements in the future.

# Women as Retirees

L AURA AND PATRICK, in their fifties, are by any measure a regular middle-class couple. Laura is a nurse. Patrick, before he developed health problems, built houses. But when Laura's mother died and willed them the family property, the IRS came after them like they were millionaires.

Laura's grandfather, her parents, and then Laura and Patrick have lived on 450 acres of land that has been in the family since the 1930s. But in 1975 Laura's dad was diagnosed with leukemia. Worried about what would happen to his wife, he sold the timber from a portion of the land and put the money into investments. He died in 1979, leaving everything to Laura's mother.

It was at that point the first estate tax nightmare began. The IRS claimed Laura's mom only had 30 percent interest in her husband's estate, leaving her to pay death taxes on the other 70 percent. The family had a long battle to get the IRS to agree to give her a 50 percent interest. Laura's mother had to use money meant for her future to pay the death tax on the other half.[1]

Time passed and Laura's mother put together a will. She started "gifting" a certain amount of her land each year to Laura and Patrick, to reduce the tax burden when she died. But she'd only managed to do this for a few years when she passed away in 1996. She left her property and $600,000 in savings to Laura and Laura's brother, Robert.

Then the estate tax nightmares started all over again. For several years, land assessors, house appraisers, and timber evaluators occupied Laura and Patrick's lives, and they watched the tax bill quickly mount. While the trees planted after the property was logged as yet had no commercial value, the IRS said that in assessing the value of the estate it would take into account the *future* commercial value of the trees. That made the estate worth more and the taxes higher.

Worse, the IRS argued that the land Laura's mother had gifted them each year had been worth more than the $10,000 she was allowed to give tax-free each year. This meant that Laura and Patrick would have to pay back taxes. By no means wealthy, Laura and Patrick looked at the huge death tax bill with dread. Yet they couldn't imagine selling their home or land that had been in Laura's family for so long, just to pay the bill.[2]

Luckily, in the end, the extra savings that Laura's mother had left just covered the taxes. "We basically had to sign over all her savings to keep the property," said Patrick. Not that this was an end to their tax difficulties. The IRS reserves the right to keep cases open for three years. And more than two years after Laura and Patrick paid the bill, the IRS came back and said they owed a further $50,000. "We really had to scratch around to find that amount," he explains.

The couple is aware that wealthier families are able to hire expensive planners and so avoid a lot of taxes and grief. "We had no experience with this. If we'd been through it three or four times we'd be old hands. But we're novices," says Patrick.

Even more frustrating is the prospect that it will never end. "They taxed Laura's mother. They taxed us. And when we die our kids will have to pay taxes on it. When do we ever get to the point where they can't take it from us anymore?"

Federal estate tax law confuses and angers people at the end of their lives, and it is but one of the ways that we treat older Americans unfairly. In many ways our nation's 35 million retirees have become second-class citizens.

The minute people hit the age of 65, they are segregated into programs that bear no relation to the rest of society. On the last day a 64-year-old woman holds a job she will pay the same taxes as her 30-year-old colleague. A month later this same woman, now retired and collecting Social Security, will face tax rates higher than those paid by millionaires Michael Jordan and Britney Spears. At the same time, she will have to withdraw from her private health insurance plan and enroll with government insurance that is distinctly inferior.

If this forced isolation weren't bad enough, nearly all of the programs "designed" for the elderly are a mess and getting messier. Take Social Security, for example. The program originally was never intended to be put to much use. In 1940, the year Social Security sent out its first, crisp benefit check, men were expected to live 61.4 years and women 65.7 years. That meant the average male could expect to die 3.6 years before he even qualified for benefits. The average female could look forward to seven whole checks. As time has passed, millions upon millions of Americans have come to depend on this government system. Today, nearly one out of every eight people in the country is over the age of 64. Medicare, by contrast, was designed at the outset (in the 1960s) for a large number of beneficiaries. But it has been unable to keep up with changes in a modern society. The bigger the program grows, the more glaring and debilitating its defects become.

Because women tend to outlive their male counterparts, the segregation into these rusting retirement relics affects them more. A tax on Social Security benefits is usually a tax on female retirees. An unfair estate tax falls disproportionately on the estates of women. A defective Medicare program means shabby health insurance for millions more women than men. And an inadequate system of long-term care means entire communities of women who live out their last years in expensive or deficient conditions.

## PROBLEM No. 1:
## PAYING TO BE OLD

The idea of a fair contract is basic to our society. And Social Security was designed to be just such a contract between the government and its citizens. The worker's part of the bargain involved paying taxes over his or her employed life. The government's obligation was to pay back these workers with benefits during retirement. Unfortunately, the terms of that contract went by the wayside long ago.

In the heady days of Social Security, when more money was coming in than was going out, the government tinkered with the contract by expanding the original benefits and even adding on new ones.[3] In recent years, as Social Security's financial prospects have darkened, the government did more tinkering—this time taking away benefits. Legislation passed in 1983, for instance, is gradually increasing the official retirement age from 65 to 67, which means future retirees will get less from the program.

More significant, in 1983 the federal government began taxing 50 percent of Social Security benefits, increasing that rate to 85 percent in 1993.[4] These taxes are a backdoor way of reducing what the government pays its senior citizens. Every extra dollar a retiree takes in (say, from a private pension or 401(k)) causes more Social Security benefits to be taxed. This puts many seniors in an impossible, Catch-22 financial situation. Even the government admits how difficult it is to survive on Social Security benefits alone. That's why there are various tax incentives to save and accumulate assets for the retirement years. But the more seniors save to supplement Social Security, the more they are punished.

The Clinton administration argued that its 1993 Social Security tax hike would only hit the "wealthiest" senior citizens. Yet guess who they considered wealthy? Single retirees pay taxes on 50 percent of their benefits to the extent that their annual income exceeds $25,000. For couples, the threshold is $32,000. A single senior need only take in $34,000 a year to start paying taxes on 85 percent of his benefits. For couples, the number is $44,000.[5]

These thresholds aren't indexed for inflation, which means that over time more and more Americans will be forced to pay these taxes even if their incomes don't increase. This is already happening. When first imposed, the taxation of Social Security benefits affected less than 10 percent of beneficiaries; today it affects one in five. By the time the children of the baby boomers retire, almost all of them will be paying tax on some portion of their benefits.

What follows is a short description of how the Social Security tax works, both for seniors who retire and for those who choose to keep working.

## Taxing Investment Income

Despite its name, the Social Security benefits tax is not really a tax on benefits. It is a tax on other income, including retirement pensions and IRA and 401(k) withdrawals. If a retiree only has Social Security, she pays no tax. But if she withdraws more than a certain amount of money from other retirement funds, she will have to pay taxes on both that extra money *and* her Social Security benefits. In exact terms, she will pay taxes on every $1 of income above the threshold, as well as taxes on 50 cents of Social Security benefits.

For simple math purposes, think of it this way: If a senior citizen receives $5,000 above the income limit, she pays taxes on the $5,000 of earnings as well as taxes on $2,500 worth of Social Security benefits. So when elderly taxpayers earn $1 they pay taxes on $1.50—making their effective tax rate 50 percent higher than otherwise.

Imagine Joan, a single senior citizen, who withdraws enough from her 401(k) to put her above the first income threshold ($25,000). On paper, Joan is in the 15 percent income tax bracket, but she pays an effective rate of 22.5 percent (15 percent × 1.5). If Joan is in the 25 percent tax bracket, she pays an effective rate of 37.5 percent (25 percent × 1.5).

Now imagine Joan wants to move to a retirement community, but to do so she must take yet more out of her 401(k). Once she goes above the second threshold ($34,000), she must pay taxes on 85 percent of her benefits for each $1 of income above that mark. For every $1 Joan takes out of her 401(k), she pays taxes on $1.85. If Joan is in the 25 percent tax bracket, she is paying an effective marginal tax rate of 46 percent (25 percent × 1.85). That means Joan faces tax rates much higher than those of her granddaughter, who takes in the exact same income.

And that's only one of the many ways the Social Security benefits tax hits retirees. It also raises the effective tax rate on capital gains and even on "tax-exempt" income (see figure 9.1). If Joan were to take income

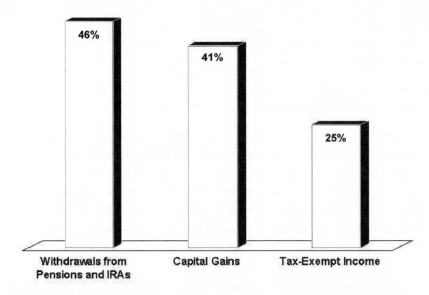

**FIGURE 9.1.** Marginal Tax Rates for the Middle Income Elderly. Assumes couples receiving Social Security benefits with income of more than $44,000, facing the Social Security benefits tax and a 25 percent federal income tax rate. (Source: For an explanation of the Social Security benefit tax and how it affects marginal tax rates, see Stephen J. Entin, "Reducing the Social Security Benefits Tax," National Center for Policy Analysis, NCPA Brief Analysis No. 332, August 2000)

from a tax-exempt bond, she would not pay tax on any interest she earns above the threshold. But the very act of receiving interest above the limit would make up to 85 cents of her benefits taxable. So if Joan were in the 25 percent tax bracket, she'd pay a tax of 21 cents on 85 cents of her benefits. She's paying a tax of 21 percent on her supposedly tax-exempt earnings! Similarly, a dollar of capital gains is taxed at the maximum rate of 20 percent. But because that dollar makes 85 cents of benefits taxable, at the 25 percent rate Joan's total effective tax rate on capital gains would be 41 percent.[6]

## Taxing Wages

The taxman is no less brutal on those senior citizens who—either out of a desire to keep busy or the need for a little extra money—remain in the labor market. A couple over the age of 65 in the 25 percent income tax bracket will not only pay the Social Security benefits tax on any income they take from savings but will also have to fork over for the payroll tax, pushing their marginal rate as high as 58.85 percent.

Then there are the unfortunate elderly who are subject to what is known as the Social Security earnings test. In general, beneficiaries past the usual Social Security retirement age of 65 can earn an unlimited amount of wages without any loss of Social Security benefits. But a heavy penalty lurks for those age 62 to 64 who choose to "retire" early and collect reduced Social Security benefits. A beneficiary in this age range loses $1 in benefits for every $2 in wage and salary income over the exempt amount ($25,000 in 2001). This is equivalent to a 50 percent tax rate. When the earnings penalty is added to other taxes, seniors can actually end up paying more in taxes than they earn in wages—a tax rate exceeding 100 percent! In this case, seniors literally pay the government for the privilege of working. As figure 9.2 shows, even beneficiaries in the 15 percent income tax bracket can face a marginal tax rate of 80.3 percent.

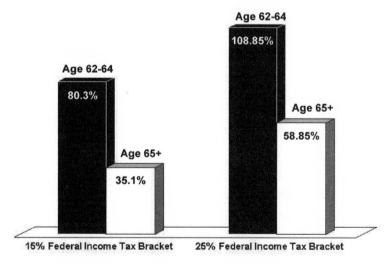

**FIGURE 9.2.** Marginal Tax Rates on Wages. (Source: Stephen J. Entin, "Reducing the Social Security Benefits Tax," National Center for Policy Analysis, NCPA Brief Analysis No. 332, August 2000)

**Benefits Tax Trap**

The Social Security benefits tax is one of the most complicated and least understood provisions in the tax code. But its effects are real and devastating, and not just limited to seniors. Many young people plunk money away into "tax-favored" accounts in the belief that by deferring taxes to their retirement years they are making a good financial decision. The sad truth is that many of this hopeful generation are simply shifting the payment of taxes to a time in their lives when they'll face the highest tax rates in the country. The Social Security benefits tax is not only unfair, it is downright sinister.

The argument for taxing Social Security benefits is that today's elderly paid far less into the Social Security program via payroll taxes than what they currently get back in benefits.[7] Even if you agree with that argument, there is a better solution and, as it happens, one that is far simpler. It makes far more sense to simply require all seniors to count a portion of their Social Security benefits as ordinary income, taxable at the same rates as younger taxpayers. That approach would be much more fair. And the program could also provide exemptions for the low-income elderly who would be hard put to pay any taxes.

## PROBLEM NO. 2:
### DYING TO PAY TAXES[8]

Few taxes in American life cause as much emotional controversy as the estate tax, also known as the death tax. Many people find it fundamentally "un-American" that the government would tax the fruits of hard work and success at the moment of death. Readers will probably know, or have heard of, families who have had to make agonizing decisions about how to pay the tax and at a time in their lives when they are already dealing with the loss of a loved one.

Compounding this, there is a very real question about the economic value of the tax. The death tax raises only a minuscule amount of money for the federal government—1.5 percent of federal revenues. And the tax has so many negative effects on economic activity that some economists believe by getting rid of it the federal government would suffer no net loss of tax revenue.[9]

At the moment the United States has the second-highest estate tax rates in the world.[10] In 2003, the first $1 million of an estate is effectively exempt from the tax, yet anything above that amount is taxed an astonishing 49 percent. Estates that fall between $10 million and $21 million face a statutory rate of 55 percent, although the tax rate people actually pay turns out to be 60 percent. And bear in mind that these rates apply to wealth that was already taxed once, when it was earned. This double taxation is one reason why polls have shown that some 90 percent of Americans think the estate tax is "unfair" and why some 70 percent want its full repeal.

What small support there is for the death tax comes from those who believe that the tax only hits the rich. But that simply isn't the case. Remember, the tax isn't on the giver but on the receiver of the estate, and those receivers don't always have much money. Consider a son who inherits the family farm from his father. The son, having worked on the struggling farm his whole life, is hardly wealthy. Yet the farm, because it encompasses a lot of real estate, is assessed at a high amount. When the father dies the son is in an impossible situation: the only way to pay the estate tax on the farm is to sell the farm itself, which means he's out of a job and a way of life.

The reality is that people of modest means are usually burdened by the estate tax, while many wealthy families avoid it completely. More than half of all estate tax revenue comes from estates under $5 million, and one study estimates that two-thirds of the wealth of the nation's richest families goes untaxed.[11]

Figure 9.3 shows that the tax rate paid by estates over $20 million is actually lower than the tax rate paid by an estate of $3 or $4 million. This gap would be even bigger if wealthier estates had only planned better. According to Columbia University economist George Cooper, "The fact that any substantial amount of tax is now being collected can be attributed only to taxpayer indifference to avoidance opportunities or a lack of aggressiveness on the part of estate planners in exploiting the loopholes that exist."[12] Brookings Institution economists Henry Aaron and Alicia Munnell have said that estate taxes aren't even taxes at all but "penalties imposed on those who neglect to plan ahead or who retain unskilled estate planners."[13]

Unfortunately, only the wealthiest individuals have the ability to plan ahead and retain the right estate planners. Clever accountants these days

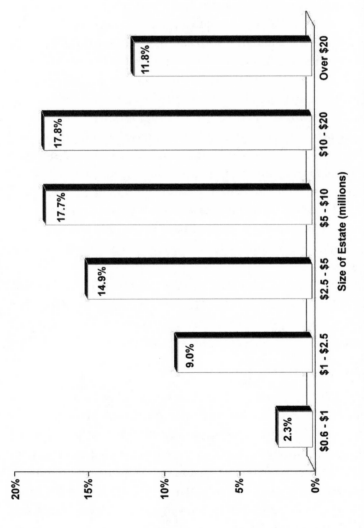

**FIGURE 9.3.** Estate Taxes as a Share of Gross Estate, 1997. (Source: Barry W. Johnson and Jacob M. Mikow, "Federal Estate Tax Returns, 1995–1997," *Statistics of Income Bulletin*, Vol. 19, Summer 1999, p. 107)

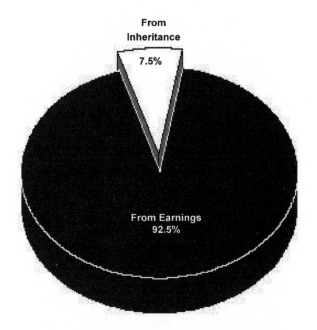

Source:   James P. Smith, *Unequal Wealth and Incentives to Save* (Santa Monica,
Calif.: Rand Corporation, 1995), p. 16.

**FIGURE 9.4.** Source of Wealth for Wealthiest 5 Percent of Americans. (Source: James P. Smith, *Unequal Wealth and Incentives to Save* [Santa Monica, Calif.: Rand Corporation, 1995], p. 16)

have at their disposal all kinds of complex tools for significantly reducing the tax burden, but it is a costly process and requires long lead times to implement. Families who have had wealth for generations are usually more familiar with these techniques and have the cash in hand to make the plans work. Most of the tax therefore falls on the backs of those who only recently acquired a small amount of wealth or who have all their money tied up in businesses that they hoped to pass along to their families. They tend to include new entrepreneurs (including many minorities), farmers, and owners of small businesses.

Another misconception about the estate tax is that it redistributes wealth across society, preventing wealthy families from passing along their fortunes from generation to generation. Yet, as figure 9.4 shows, very few of the assets of the wealthiest Americans actually come from inheritance.

The worst part of the estate tax is that it is unfair in principle. Those who get stuck paying it were already taxed once on their estates—when their money was earned. If they then went on to invest that money in a business it would have been taxed several more times: through the corporate income tax, the personal income tax on dividends and interest income, and the capital gains tax when shares of stock in the company were sold. The estate tax, through which the government seizes more than half of anything left after this prior tax-fest, is just one more way of socking it to people who saved and invested rather than consumed everything during their lifetime.

President George W. Bush's tax cut of 2001 grants some relief. The top estate tax rate will fall from 49 percent in 2003 to 48 percent in 2004 and gradually decline to 45 percent in 2009. In 2010, it will be repealed completely. But thanks to congressional shenanigans, the tax will only disappear for one year. It will be reinstated completely in 2011—reverting again to a top rate of 55 percent. Needless to say, the elderly and their families have been left to wonder how to plan for the future. More than a few senior citizens have morbidly noted that if they are going to die they hope to have the good fortune to do it during the one-year grace period. Far better would be a long-term policy that removed the burden of the estate tax once and for all.

## PROBLEM NO. 3:
## MEDICARE MAYHEM

One of the strange realities of modern America is that Medicare remains a politically popular program despite the fact it violates nearly every principle of sound insurance policy. It pays too many small bills that the elderly could easily afford to pay themselves, while sticking them with thousands of dollars of out-of-pocket expenses, including the cost of most prescription drugs. Each year about 750,000 Medicare beneficiaries spend more than $5,000 of their own funds for health care.[14]

We can mark some of these defects down to an outdated design. In the beginning, Medicare was modeled on the standard Blue Cross plan, popular in 1965. But as Blue Cross and other private insurers updated their structures and policies to deal with modern medicine, Medicare, a creature of politics, gathered dust. The program is still caught in a 1960s time warp, which means most seniors are in an insurance program that is far inferior to those used by the rest of the nation.

America's seniors are fully aware of many of Medicare's shortcomings, which is the reason two-thirds of them acquire supplemental insurance—either through a former employer or through direct purchase. Although these "Medigap" policies are designed to plug the holes in Medicare, most don't cover prescriptions, and even those that do often have only spotty coverage. Oddly enough, the only seniors who do qualify for good drug coverage are those poor enough to qualify for Medicaid, a federal-state health program for the low-income.

This hodgepodge of Medicare, Medicaid, and Medigap policies leads to a great deal of waste. In fact, health economists estimate that seniors with both Medicare and Medigap insurance spend about 30 percent more on health care than those with Medicare alone.[15] Plus, patients without drug coverage often turn to more expensive (and often less effective) doctor or physician therapies instead. Ironically, Medicare will pay for the hospital costs of a stroke victim but won't pay for the drugs that would have prevented the stroke in the first place. It will pay to amputate the leg of a diabetic but not for the chronic care that would have made the amputation unnecessary.

At President Bush's urging, Congress has recently created a new Medicare program, with a separate premium, to cover prescription drugs. Although this change will create extra benefits for millions of seniors, it will do so in a wasteful way. The elderly are the only people in our society who routinely pay two premiums to two plans. Soon they will pay three premiums to three plans. What they really need is one premium for one plan that covers all their health-care needs.

Start by combining the amount Medicare spends on the elderly with the money they currently spend on private insurance. That would be enough to allow seniors to buy the same kind of health insurance younger people have, including coverage for prescription drugs, according to a study prepared for the National Center for Policy Analysis by Milliman & Robertson, Inc., the nation's leading actuarial firm on health benefits.[16]

Congress thought it was allowing seniors to use their Medicare money to join private health plans when it passed Medicare+Choice in 1997. The program was supposed to give the elderly the full range of health insurance options currently available to non-seniors, including health maintenance organizations, medical savings accounts, fee-for-service plans, doctor-run plans, and more. This might have all worked out well if the Health Care Financing Administration (HCFA), the agency that regulates Medicare, hadn't been determined to throw wrenches in the works. From the beginning, HCFA was hostile to private insurance, hostile to competition, and hostile to choice. The agency saddled the new Medicare option with so many rules and regulations that seniors have few of the options they were originally promised.

As a result, only 11 percent of Medicare beneficiaries are today enrolled in Medicare+Choice plans, down from 16 percent in 1999.[17] That's too bad, because these private plans were providing comprehensive coverage (often including drug coverage) to seniors who were trying to survive on Medicare alone. The new Medicare bill is supposed to reverse the trend. In fact the White House predicts that by 2009, up to one-third of seniors will be enrolled in private plans that resemble the insurance the rest of America has. Let's hope they are right.

## PROBLEM NO. 4: A LONG-TERM MESS

No one likes to think about the day when a relative they know and love is no longer able to live on her own. That day brings with it the trauma of moving a person out of her lifelong home, of watching her give up self-sufficiency, and sometimes of confronting a disease that needs professional attention. Yet as the elderly start to live longer, that is a prospect more of us will face.

In fact, long-term care in the United States is a train wreck waiting to happen. On the average, the elderly have a 43 percent chance of entering a nursing home during their lifetimes. Some 9 percent of seniors can expect to spend five years or more in such a facility. The costs are often staggering.[18]

One reason for the high costs is too much regulation. Federal fire, health, and safety regulations mean that most nursing homes can withstand natural disasters that would knock down most luxury hotels. These and other regulations have made the average stay in a nursing home run close to $66,000 a year.[19]

Who pays for this? You might be forgiven for thinking that Medicare—the program specifically designed to look after the health of the elderly—foots the bill. Not so. Most nursing home expenses are paid by seniors themselves. And once their savings are exhausted, Medicaid (the health program for the poor) starts picking up the bill.[20] Medicare chips in only 2 percent of the costs, and private insurance pays for less than 1 percent.

Long-term residents of nursing homes therefore fall eventually into one of two categories: they are either relatively wealthy (and can pay themselves) or extremely poor (and thus qualify for Medicaid). And most of the elderly who are officially "poor" only recently became so. Half of nursing home residents covered by Medicaid did not qualify for Medicaid when they arrived at the facility. They only became eligible after depleting their own financial resources.

Perhaps more disturbing is the news that for every elderly person in a nursing home today there are two more *equally disabled* patients who are not in nursing homes. Yet expanding Medicare coverage even slightly to include more nursing home care could easily wipe out the entire program. If every elderly person spent just one year in a nursing home, the cost would be close to $2 trillion. To put that in perspective, that's almost as large as the federal budget. It's also more than the entire country spends on all health care each year.[21]

So what's the answer? One problem is that the federal government does very little to encourage average citizens to plan and save for their own long-term care costs. Although most people get a generous tax subsidy for their current health insurance, people cannot deduct the cost of long-term care insurance premiums. Federal tax policy is encouraging us to overinsure for today's health needs and underinsure for tomorrow's. Also, prior to recently passed legislation, most people could not contribute to Health Savings Accounts that grow over time and provide a source of funds for long-term care. President Bush has proposed tax incentives to help families meet their own long-term care needs and provide care for elderly family members, but these are baby steps.[22]

Another difficulty is that elderly entitlement programs are overly compartmentalized. Senior citizens have well-defined benefit rights under Social Security, well-defined benefit rights under Medicare, and well-defined benefit rights under Medicaid. But the benefits are rigid and in general cannot substitute for each other. Medicare funds (for the most part) cannot be used for long-term care in a facility and they cannot be used at all for ordinary living expenses. Similarly, Medicaid's long-term care funds cannot in general be used for home living.

Notice how different the federal government's approach is from what seniors themselves are doing. The idea behind "assisted living" communities is that living expenses, health-care expenses, and long-term care expenses need to be integrated, not compartmentalized. Seniors in these communities usually have onsite access to primary care. As they age, they can take advantage of increased levels of "assistance." To 7.5 million Americans with functional limitations over the age of 65, access to personal assistance services makes the difference between a full life and one of decrepitude. The demand for an integrated approach is so large that assisted living communities are cropping up all over the country and are undoubtedly the wave of the future. By contrast, our federal programs are mired in the past.[23]

As with everything we've examined in this book, failures of public policy hurt men as well as women. But because women live longer, they are more likely to experience the defects of Medicare and Medicaid, including gaps in coverage and arbitrary restrictions. And because younger women tend to be the primary caregivers in families, they are more likely to bear the burden when Medicare or Medicaid fails to meet the needs of a senior parent. Until the federal government overhauls Social Security benefit taxes, the estate tax, Medicare, and long-term care, a growing number of seniors will be denied those "golden years."

┌─────────┐
│   10    │
│    ~    │
└─────────┘

# WOMEN AND THE FUTURE
# OF ELDERLY ENTITLEMENT
# PROGRAMS

B ETH MAY ONLY be 28 years old, but the New York-
based writer already spends a fair amount of time thinking about the day when she retires. And for as much as
she follows the ongoing debates about the future of Social Security, she's
already come to a few conclusions. If the federal retirement program continues to operate the way it does now, "I don't expect I'll be getting anything near what today's senior citizens get," she says. "And even if I do get
something it will be with the knowledge that I'm making the younger
generation pay for me. It's a house of cards."

Beth is just one of many young Americans who have lost faith that
the government will be there to provide for them when they leave the
workforce. She's concerned enough about her future that she's saving for
her own retirement. Beth makes a point of putting the maximum personal amount into her company-provided 401(k) plan each year, and also
tries to sock away $2,000 a year into an IRA. Still, she recognizes that
many in her generation don't have the ability to do the same. And she

wonders if she'll always be able to make that financial commitment. "Right now I have no excuses—I don't have a husband; I don't have dependents."

Not that saving has been entirely easy or gratifying to Beth. She put her first $1,800 into an IRA in 1998. The market was roaring and she took the advice that young people should invest money aggressively. But the later market collapse took the air out of her personal investment bubble; today her original $1,800 is worth $500. She remembers how she'd get online to watch the decline and "just worry and worry." She finally spoke to her father, who lectured that "if I wasn't adult enough to watch the market go up and down and not touch the money, then I shouldn't look at all. I stopped looking. But it's still hard."

Beth believes that Social Security has an obligation to keep the current system in place for those people currently edging toward retirement, but she wants the program to start giving younger folks like her more control. In particular, she likes the idea of giving people access to private Social Security accounts. "It would accomplish all kinds of good things. It would let people earn more than what Social Security promises. It would also cause us to face the fact that we are going to have to provide for our own retirements," she says. Beth not only wants this to happen soon, she also wants the government to allow her to divert a significant portion of her payroll taxes into one of these accounts. "Let's face it," she says, "Washington is a pretty unsafe place for anyone to put her money."

Imagine a bathtub with a broken plug. No matter how much water you run in from the tap, more runs out through the drain—making it impossible to get a really good soak. That's the best way to describe the future funding of Social Security and Medicare. Right now, the two programs combined are collecting a bit more in taxes than they are paying out in benefits. But once the baby boomers start to retire, the deficits will start to soar. At that point, the government will no longer be able to maintain full benefit payments to future retirees like Beth at current tax rates.

If the government does want to continue fulfilling its promises to retirees, it will have to demand an ever-increasing portion of workers' incomes. In fact, if current trends continue, by 2030 we will either have to double the payroll tax (from 15 to 30 percent) or cut every entitlement program in half.

Three reasons exist for this future messy state, and each one relates to women more than men. First, people (and women in particular) are living longer and collecting more Social Security checks. Second, medical care is becoming more expensive, and seniors (especially women) are consuming more of it. Third, women in the United States (and, indeed, all over the world) are having fewer children.

This last fact means that the number of retirees is growing faster than the number of new workers (see figure 10.1). When Social Security first started issuing payments in 1940, the country had 42 workers paying into the system for every one senior receiving a check. Today, there are slightly more than three workers paying taxes for every senior collecting benefits. By the middle of this century, when today's teenagers reach their golden years, the ratio will be close to 2 to 1.[1]

You don't have to be a mathematician to see where this will lead. If there are 10 workers for one retiree, each might only have to give 10 percent of her earnings to support that older person. Cut the number to five

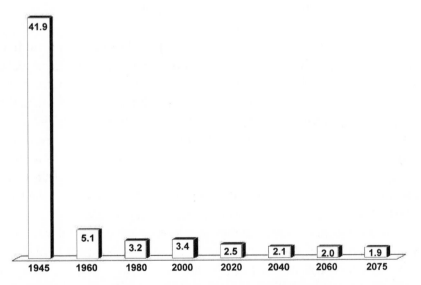

**FIGURE 10.1.** Number of Workers Per Retiree. Figures for 1945 through 2000 are actual. Figures for 2020 through 2075 are intermediate projections. (Source: *2001 Annual Report of the Board of Trustees of the Federal Old-Age and Survivors Insurance and Disability Insurance Trust Funds, Intermediate Projection.*)

workers, however, and each must give 20 percent to support the same senior at the same level of benefits. Slash the number to two and each worker is paying close to 50 percent of his salary for the older generation. Or at least, that's how it would work out if seniors were totally dependent on young taxpayers and enjoyed the same standard of living.

Beth's own family is a perfect example of this number crunch. Beth's grandfathers were each one of 11 siblings. Her mother and father, in contrast, came from families of five and three. And while neither Beth nor her two siblings are yet married, she sees only "two, maybe three" kids in her own future. Families are simply getting smaller. But fewer workers per retiree mean fewer taxpayers per retiree. This in turn forces a choice: a higher tax burden for workers or lower benefits for seniors.

## PROBLEM NO. 1:
## BYE-BYE BABIES

Given all the new and revolutionary fertility treatments in the Western world, you might think women are bearing children at unprecedented rates. Quite the opposite is true.

The definition of a country's fertility rate is the number of children a woman will produce over a lifetime, on the average (see figure 10.2). In order for a developed nation to replace its population, it needs a fertility rate of about 2.1.[2] Today's U.S. fertility rate is 2.07—higher than the low of 1.8 in 1976 but still not enough to replace the current generation. And the U.S. number is greater than that of most other developed nations. The average fertility rate for Europe is 1.4. Germany stands at 1.3 and Italy clocks in at just 1.2. The world has never seen fertility rates this low, and it isn't a passing fad. A falling fertility rate has been the hallmark of much of the world for more than a half century.

These numbers, benign as they may look on paper, have devastating implications for the future. A low fertility rate means that the total number of residents will eventually peak and then begin to shrink. The Social Security Administration's own "pessimistic" projection forecasts that the U.S. population will peak about the middle of this century. If that forecast holds true, the U.S. population one hundred years from now will be about the same size it is today but with one major difference: it will be a

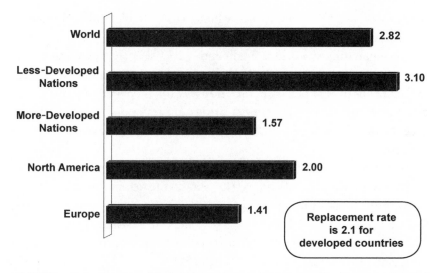

**FIGURE 10.2.** Average Births Per Woman (1995-2000). (Source: "World Population Prospects: The 2000 Revision," United Nations Population Division, www.un.org/esa/population/wpp2000/wpp2000h.pdf)

whole lot older. The number of old people relative to the number of young will continue to grow continuously, as will the tax burden on the younger workers.

## PROBLEM NO. 2:
## NOT PAYING-AS-WE-GO

Contrary to a lot of misleading rhetoric (much of it unfortunately found in Social Security Administration pamphlets), our elderly entitlement programs are not funded. In a funded system, workers put away funds for safekeeping to use during their own retirement.

Social Security and Medicare are instead pay-as-you-go programs, which means today's workers pay for today's seniors. Every dollar collected in payroll (FICA) taxes is spent—the very day, the hour, the minute it comes in the door. Most of this tax money pays Social Security benefits and Medicare expenses. Anything left over is whisked away by politicians to fund other federal programs or to pay off the national debt.

Nothing is saved. No money is stashed away in bank vaults. No investments are made in the stock market or other assets.

So when today's workers finally retire, they will be dependent on the next generation for their own retirement and health benefits. Only there will be fewer of that next generation to pay up. If we keep a pay-as-you-go system, the options are very clear: Future retirees will either have to accept lower benefits, or the younger generation will have to pay more in taxes.

In order for the government to keep its promises, how high will future taxes have to be? As figure 10.3 shows, the tax rates needed to support multiplying numbers of elderly are on course to soar.[3] Today, the payroll tax rate for Social Security retirement and disability insurance is 12.4 percent, nothing to sneeze at if you consider all the federal, state, and local income taxes we are also expected to pay. Yet that number will hit 17 percent by the time today's teenagers reach retirement age in 2050.[4]

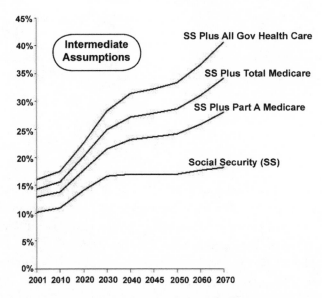

**FIGURE 10.3.** Elderly Entitlement Spending As a Percent of Taxable Payroll. (Source: National Center for Policy Analysis calculations and *2002 Annual Report of the Board of Trustees of the Federal Old-Age and Survivors Insurance and Disability Insurance Trust Funds.*)

And that's only for starters. When one adds in Medicare Part A (which covers hospital expenses) the needed payroll tax rate will hit 24 percent by mid-century. Medicare Part B (which covers outpatient services) is funded from general tax revenues; but if we were to express the benefits as a percent of payroll, the tax rate would climb to 28 percent. And if we add in the other ways in which the federal government pays elderly medical bills (Medicaid, the Veterans Administration, etc.), the total tax burden bumps up against 33 percent.

Considering how resistant much of today's generation is to paying higher taxes, imagine how future workers will react to the prospect of delivering nearly one-third of their incomes to pay seniors' benefits already enshrined in law. That burden will come on top of everything else people expect from government, including roads and bridges, schools and police, and national defense. These forecasts also don't include Congress's recent decision to add a costly new Medicare prescription drug benefit.

Further, this is a relatively rosy view of how things will turn out. All these numbers are based on the intermediate (most likely) projections of the Social Security Board of Trustees. Under the trustees' pessimistic projection, by 2050 the total taxes needed to support elderly benefits will climb to 54.4 percent of taxable payroll. Under this scenario, we have already pledged more than half of the incomes of future workers—most of whom haven't even been born and who have not agreed to be part of this chain-letter approach to funding retirement benefits.

## WHAT TRUST FUNDS?

Any discussion of Social Security must address the "trust funds." Is there somewhere, hidden from the public's view, a whole lot of cash stashed away for the benefit of future retirees? Unfortunately, no.

It is true that Social Security, Disability Insurance, and Medicare Part A technically have trust funds. But these funds serve no economic function. They exist purely for accounting purposes, to keep track of the inflow and outflow of funds. For example, the trust fund balance for Social Security shows the cumulative difference between the amount of payroll taxes that have come in and the benefits that have been paid out.

Yet just because the trust fund shows a "surplus" on paper doesn't mean there's any money sitting around. As mentioned, extra funds are spent on other projects. The Social Security trust funds do not receive any money or spend any money. Every payroll tax check written by employers is written to the U.S. Treasury and every Social Security benefit check comes from the U.S. Treasury.

So what exactly is in the trust funds? The filing cabinets of the Social Security offices in Parkersburg, West Virginia, are stuffed full of certificates that are supposed to represent trust fund surpluses. But these nonnegotiable bonds can't be sold on Wall Street or to foreign investors. In essence, they are nothing more than IOUs the government writes to itself in order to keep a running tab of how much Social Security money it spends on other things.

On paper, the Social Security trust funds have enough IOUs to "pay" Social Security benefits for about three years, and the Medicare trust fund to "pay" benefits for a little more than two years. In practice, Social Security can only hand these IOUs back to the Treasury and ask the Treasury to pay benefits. But since the Treasury doesn't have any money set aside to pay for three years of Social Security or two years of Medicare, the only way it could do so is if Congress authorizes more taxing or borrowing. No Social Security benefit can actually be paid with IOUs the government has written to itself.

If the trust funds were abolished tomorrow, no one would notice a thing. The government would not be relieved of any of its existing obligations or commitments. Similarly, if a presidential executive order could, with the stroke of a pen, double or triple the number of IOUs in the trust fund, that also would make no difference. Yet either option would be preferable to today's misguided perception that somehow the trust funds will play a role in meeting Social Security obligations. The only real question is how the Treasury is going to pay future retirement bills.

## Moving to a Funded System

The alternative to a pay-as-you-go system is a funded system. In a funded program, payroll tax contributions are saved and invested, so that each generation of workers has the money to pay for its own retirement benefits. Retirees don't depend on younger generations. Instead, they pay their own way.

In some countries, such as Singapore, Social Security has always been a funded system. Others, such as Chile, began with a pay-as-you-go system similar to ours and then transformed it (in 1981) into a funded system. Still others, Britain for instance, have a mixed retirement system—part funded and part pay-as-you-go. The decision to adopt a funded system is a decision to avoid the problems that plague most other countries in the world today. Countries with funded systems don't have to worry about how many children women are going to bear or how big a tax burden will be faced by our children and grandchildren.[5]

Most of today's proposals for reforming Social Security involve moving toward a funded system, in particular allowing today's younger workers to begin investing a portion of their payroll taxes in personal retirement accounts that could be used for their own golden years. Over time these personal accounts would grow, replacing a bigger and bigger portion of the government's Social Security burden. History shows that long-term investments in capital markets are likely to provide a higher return than what Social Security promises—even assuming those promises are kept. This, in turn, means a safer retirement for millions of workers.

President Bush's Commission to Strengthen Social Security considered a number of different proposals.[6] One, made by the National Center for Policy Analysis (NCPA), would work like this:[7] During their years on the job, workers would divert 2 percent of the payroll they currently pay in taxes into their own private retirement account. When they retire, each of these workers would receive two checks, one from that private account and another from the traditional government program. Key to all this is a government promise that workers would get a payout at least as large as the one offered under the current government-only system. That means workers have nothing to lose from trying the new funded system. At the very least, they'll get what they are currently being promised. Most, however, would enjoy the much larger fruits of many years of private investment.

## OVERCOMING THE FEAR FACTOR

Public opinion polls show that replacing Social Security with private retirement accounts is very popular, especially among young people. A recent poll conducted for NCPA by Public Opinion Strategies found that 80 percent of Generation X voters say they would switch to a personal retirement account plan if given the option.[8] But the polls also show some groups are more nervous than others. Women, for instance, are less enthusiastic about personal accounts than men. It's normal to have worries about retirement safety, but on closer inspection most of these worries are overblown.

### What if People Don't Save?

Under all serious proposals in the United States, workers would be *required* to put money into personal accounts. Just as employers today are forced to withhold payroll taxes from employees' wages, match them, and then make payments to the government, a reformed system would require deposits to private accounts. Anyone who didn't would face criminal penalties for a failure to comply.

### What if People Don't Make Good Investment Decisions?

This is perhaps the biggest worry that workers have about a private system, as the case of Beth shows. Most Americans have read horror stories about Enron employees who lost everything when they invested all of their money in their employer's stock. But the reform proposals under consideration in the United States, as well as the experiences of other countries, show that this doesn't have to be a concern.

Chile was the first nation in the Western Hemisphere to establish a Social Security system, as well as the first nation in the modern era to then completely privatize its system. While the average Chilean has a choice between two dozen companies to manage her private retirement account, these investment funds operate under specific ground rules. Most important of these is that every fund must hold a broad-based portfolio that reflects the Chilean market as a whole. Similarly, the NCPA recommends that private retirement accounts in the United States be required to invest in portfolios that reflect the market as a whole. Consequently, individuals won't be picking individual stocks and can't be ruined by one-week wonders or risky stocks that go bust. Unlike 401(k) accounts, people with Social Security private retirement accounts would not have the opportunity to be either too conservative or too risky.

### What If the Market Crashes the Day before You Retire?

Markets go up and down over time, so it is always possible that a person's private account will be hit by a downturn at the exact moment of retirement. Yet even factoring in this unlikely scenario, almost anyone under age 65 today would still have been better off if they'd been investing their Social Security taxes in the stock market. That would be the case even if on the day before your retirement the market took a plunge by as much as it did on the worst day in its entire history.[9]

As an added security, individuals would be encouraged to move to a more conservative portfolio as they aged and neared retirement. The government should also make the aforementioned guarantee that nobody would be worse off with a private retirement account than she would be under the current system. This is a promise the government can easily afford to make, especially as its long-term funding problems disappear over time because of the growth of the private accounts.

### Are the Administrative Costs of a Private System Too High?

If reformers design the system the right way, administrative costs can be kept quite low. Today, for example, the federal government gives federal employees private investment options, and that program's administrative costs are a low 0.09 percent. Based on research by the investment firm State Street Global Advisors, the NCPA has shown that a national system of private retirement accounts can be administered for no more than 0.2 percentage points.[10]

### How Would Benefits Be Paid during the Retirement Years?

Under the NCPA proposal, individuals would use their account balances to purchase variable annuities during their retirement years. The annuity companies would invest in broad-based portfolios and be required to keep administrative costs low. Each month the retiree would receive a private annuity check, as well as a traditional check from the federal government.

## How Would the Reformed System Affect Women?

Social Security reform has become so popular that proposals are flooding in from all quarters. But not all are as good for women as others. Any true Social Security reform, for instance, needs to address the dilemmas of divorce and the low return paid to the second earner in working families. As discussed in chapter 9, many women who get divorced before 10 years qualify for no Social Security whatsoever. And married women workers often get little, if any, benefit from years of paying payroll taxes.

On top of this, any reform needs to take account of the difference in the investment behavior of men and women. As we discuss in chapter 9, many women tend to invest too conservatively when given the choice. This makes it impossible for them to amass a big enough retirement egg. Then again, some women face the risk of a meager retirement if their husband's investments are *too* risky.

These problems are surmountable. An NCPA study of Social Security reforms in Argentina, Chile, and Mexico found that women were the biggest winners as a result of the reforms.[11] In addition to private accounts, the NCPA proposal calls for earnings sharing. All deposits would be shared equally between husband and wife, regardless of who earns the income. And again, the federal government would ensure that spouses would not be worse off under the new system than they would be under the old.

## WHAT CAN BE DONE?

In general, reform should follow these principles:[12]

- The nation should move as quickly as possible to a funded system, one in which each generation pays for its own retirement.

- Workers should be able to invest part of their payroll taxes through a private account.
- Investment choices should be limited to broad-based portfolios that reflect the general growth of the economy over the years.
- Even with private retirement accounts, government needs to make a guarantee: Nobody should be worse off than he or she would be with the current pay-as-you-go model.
- Deposits to private retirement accounts must include earnings sharing. The deposits should be equally split between the accounts of husbands and wives, regardless of who earns the money or the difference between their wages.
- Even with earnings sharing, women must get a government promise that they won't be worse off under a new system than they are under the old.

# WOMEN AND WELFARE

O SHANETTE NEAL[1] didn't have the sort of early life many people would envy. She didn't know her father. Her mother was a drug addict who occasionally went to prison and always received welfare. When Oshanette was 13, Social Services took her and her six siblings away from her mother. The siblings went to a relative in Tennessee, but Oshanette stayed behind in Denver to be close to her mother. She lived with relatives who were also on welfare.

Oshanette was 16 when she had her first child and 17 when she first hit the welfare rolls. Over the next 11 years she had five more children. Of the four different men who fathered these babies, one is a gang member, another is in a federal penitentiary, and none pays child support. Over all those years, Oshanette remained on welfare.

She might still be getting assistance were it not for reforms that went into effect in Colorado in 1997. By 2002, Oshanette had reached the new five-year limit on benefits and had to find a job. Since then she's been working a $7-an-hour job as a teacher's aide in a daycare center run by a church. She brings home $960 a month, about $300 more than she did on welfare. She's no longer a welfare "lifer."

Not that everything is perfect. Oshanette still lives below the poverty level and receives Medicaid, $517 a month in food stamps, and lives in a subsidized apartment. She faces difficulties with childcare. But now that she's off welfare, she says she would like to get off food stamps and Medicaid as well. At night she prays that God will help her to find a job that offers benefits and opportunity for advancement.

When asked how hard it will be for Oshanette to keep her children from repeating the pattern of her own life, to break the welfare cycle, she answers: "I have already broken it. I have shown my kids that you can get up and go to work and have a family. I'm showing them you have to earn your way in life. My mother was in and out of the house a lot but she always knew that welfare check would be there for her. There was no one to set an example for me. I've changed that for my family. I am the example and I'm doing all I can to be a good one."

If there's one program that has come to signify the failure of the social safety net, it's welfare. The stories of young men and women who became hooked intravenously to the government drip of welfare assistance became so infamous that Congress was moved to enact major overhaul of the program in 1996. It was one of the few times that politicians have agreed to fundamentally reform a major entitlement program.

Welfare, like so many of today's social programs, was built in a different sort of America. The federal government had always assumed that single motherhood would be temporary. It believed families would look after their own. And it held on for many years to the heady idea that it was possible to create generous entitlement benefits without adverse consequences.

Those assumptions weren't too far off the mark for most of the century. In the early 1900s, 46 of 48 states established public welfare programs for "deserving" poor single mothers, mainly widows with children. In 1935, the programs began receiving federal funding at the urging of President Franklin D. Roosevelt and support expanded over time. By 1965, President Lyndon B. Johnson's War on Poverty had created Aid to Families with Dependent Children—the main source of cash welfare until recently.[2]

But President Johnson's poverty war wasn't all that was happening in 1960s America. Prior to then, there had been a stigma attached to receiving welfare. Families often went hungry just to avoid the embarrassment of standing in line for a dole check. And very few young women in the early part of the 20th century dared to break the social taboo of having children out of wedlock.

By the 1960s, however, these traditional attitudes were being swept away. Never again would they exert the same influence on behavior. In 1940, less than 4 percent of births were to unmarried women. In 2000, more than one-third of all of births were to unmarried women.[3]

With the stigma gone, people became increasingly free to respond to economic incentives. During the first few years of the War on Poverty, the poverty rate declined and it looked as though the program was working. But by the 1970s, all had changed. Under Presidents Richard Nixon and Gerald Ford, welfare standards were liberalized (often by executive order) and spending shot up. The more we spent, the worse things got. The number of people living in poverty began steadily rising, to the point that it became obvious to scholars and the general public alike that we were paying people to be poor.

## PROBLEM NO. 1:
## STAYING POOR

By the time President Bill Clinton took his oath of office in 1992, the United States had spent $5 trillion on the War on Poverty. What success did we have? The poverty rate was higher that year than it was in 1965 when Johnson's War on Poverty began. In the intervening years, the country had benefited from economic growth and rising incomes. Yet although we spent more on poverty programs than we did on national defense, the ranks of the poor kept right on multiplying.

By 1992, there were at least 79 welfare programs. Federal and state governments spent at least $305 billion on the effort in that year alone. Moreover, because most of these programs were interrelated and overlapping, they were also wasteful. If we had simply taken all the welfare dollars we flushed through these bureaucracies and instead handed them directly to those below the poverty level, we could have given every poor person in America $8,939 in 2002. That would have equaled $35,756 for a family of four—more than the average family income for the population as a whole at the time.[4]

Worse, there's no evidence that taxpayers got anything in return for all this money. A 1989 simulation by the President's Council of Economic Advisers attempted to estimate what the poverty rate would have been if we hadn't had any federal welfare programs but had simply relied on economic growth to lift peoples' fortunes. The conclusion: economic growth alone would have reduced the poverty rate to a level about the same as, or even lower than, the one we actually had.[5]

## PROBLEM NO. 2:
## SPENDING MONEY AND NOT GETTING RESULTS

How is it possible to spend enormous sums of money and still fail to reduce the amount of poverty? Simple. The official poverty counters looked only at cash income in deciding who was poor. Yet welfare became increasingly attractive because of such in-kind (noncash) benefits as medical care, food stamps, and public housing. Welfare recipients got more and more of these in-kind benefits yet, at least on paper, remained officially "poor." From 1972 to 1993, total cash transfers to the poor barely changed in real terms. Yet over the same period, total welfare spending almost tripled.[6]

This boom in in-kind benefits also meant that most of the money we spent didn't go to poor people but to those employed in the welfare-poverty industry. Medicaid dollars went to doctors and hospitals. Food stamp dollars went to the agricultural industry. Housing subsidies went to landlords. Legal service dollars went to lawyers. So long as the bureaucrats only looked at cash disbursements—and not at the unlimited amounts of food, shelter, and medical care—it was easy to still classify most welfare recipients as "poor."

But were they really poor? By most other measures (outside of cash transfers) most welfare recipients weren't as bad off as you might think. According to Census Bureau estimates, households in the bottom 20 percent (when ranked by income) were spending $2.30 for every $1 of reported income.[7] America's "poor" may not have been living like kings, but they also weren't destitute. A Heritage Foundation investigation in the 1990s found that the average "poor" American was living in a larger house or apartment, was more likely to own a car, and was more likely to have basic amenities such as an indoor toilet than the general population of Western Europe.

In addition, some 53 percent of "poor" households had air-conditioning. Another 91 percent owned a color television, while more than 29 percent owned two or more. Nearly two-thirds owned a car (14 percent owned two or more vehicles) and 56 percent owned a microwave. Most astounding, 40 percent of the official "poor" owned their own home, with 71,000 claiming houses worth more than $300,000.[8]

Most of America's poor also weren't suffering from any of the real worries of scarcity. Poverty-induced malnutrition, for instance, was almost nonexistent in the United States. Those living below the poverty line had essentially the same level of nutritional intake as the middle class. They were more likely to suffer from obesity than from hunger.[9]

In addition to spending exorbitant amounts on in-kind benefits, our welfare programs threw a lot of money at the wrong people. Most Americans would like to believe that their welfare dollars are going to the people who need it most. Yet one of the least-known facts about America's 30-year War on Poverty is what a poor job it did in directing help to the truly needy.

A federal report in the mid-1980s concluded that only 41 percent of all poverty families were receiving food stamps. Yet of those who were, 28 percent had incomes above the poverty level. About 23 percent of poverty families were living in public housing or receiving housing subsidies; yet almost half of families receiving these benefits were not poor. Medicaid covered 40 percent of poverty families, yet 40 percent of all Medicaid beneficiaries were not in poverty.[10]

In total, 41 percent of poor families were receiving no means-tested benefit of any kind from government. Yet more than half of all families who did receive at least one means-tested benefit were not poor.

## PROBLEM NO. 3:
## PENALTIES FOR LEAVING WELFARE AND GOING TO WORK

By the time the United States had rolled into the early 1990s, welfare hadn't just attracted millions of low-income people to government aid—it had given them dozens of reasons to keep on collecting. Single mothers saw little upside to leaving the system. If they got a job, they not only lost their welfare benefits, but had to pay income and payroll taxes. And more work meant fewer Earned Income Tax Credit benefits. All told, low-income families leaving welfare faced some of the highest marginal tax rates found anywhere in the economy.

New York University Law School tax specialist Daniel Shapiro calculated the penalties levied on single welfare mothers who got a job.[11] He found that a single mother with two children in a high welfare benefit state faced a 90 percent marginal tax rate if she went to work (see figure 11.1). In return for earning the minimum wage of $5.15 an hour, she'd keep only 10 cents of each dollar she earned (factoring in both taxes and forgone benefits). If she moved up the income ladder and made a wage of $6.43 an hour, her marginal tax rate became 109 percent. For every dollar she earned, she lost a dollar and nine cents.

Even in states with low welfare benefits the taxes became exorbitant, beginning with a 58 percent marginal rate at the minimum wage and

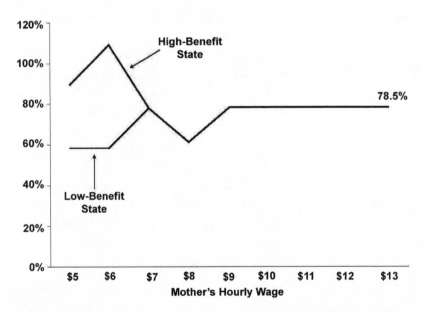

**FIGURE 11.1.** Marginal Tax Rates for a Single Mother with Two Children. (Source: Daniel N. Shapiro, "Effective Marginal Tax Rates on Low-Income Households," Employment Policies Institute, February 1999)

rising as a woman developed skills and earned more money. No wonder so many women with children chose welfare over work, given the options. Most women weren't able to "afford" to take a job and succeed on their own.

## PROBLEM NO. 4:
## ONE-SIZE-FITS-ALL WELFARE

America's private sector knows that it doesn't pay to lump all people into the same categories. Different workers respond to different types of incentives. Different consumers respond to different kinds of advertising and prices.

Government is sometimes slow on the uptake, and one of welfare's biggest problems was that it treated all of the "poor" in the exact same way, ignoring their many differences. Mary Jo Bane and David Ellwood of Harvard University conducted one of the more fascinating studies on this subject. The researchers found striking differences as to why people became poor, how long they remained poor, and how they ceased to be poor.[12] Their findings help to explain why the poverty population as a whole is so difficult to pigeonhole.

Bane and Ellwood's way of explaining the differences was to compare the poverty population to patients in a hospital. If you were to look only at admissions, it would appear that the majority of patients stay in a hospital for only a short time. You might then conclude that there is no real problem with long-term hospitalization. But if you look at all the patients occupying hospital beds on any given day, you will see that the chronic patients (whose stays are long) occupy a large portion of the beds. In other words, the chronically ill account for a small fraction of hospital *admissions*, but they occupy a large fraction of hospital *beds*.

The same is true for welfare. If you looked only at the "admission rate" of poor people to welfare rolls, it would seem that we don't have much of a welfare problem. Researchers have found that among people who become poor at any one time, 45 percent are usually out of poverty within one year. Almost 70 percent are out of poverty within three years. Only about 12 percent remain in poverty for 10 years or more.[13]

But this ignores the fact that there are a significant number of people who have been in the welfare system a long time and remain there a long time. These long-term recipients are, to use the hospital analogy, the chronically ill. Researchers found that among people receiving Aid to Families with Dependent Children (AFDC), more than half remained in poverty for 10 years or more.[14] The average black child in poverty remained on AFDC for almost two decades.[15]

Bane and Ellwood also discovered that even the short-term poor differ radically in the reasons for their poverty and in the ways they get out of poverty. These differences are important. To go back to the hospital analogy, no doctor in his right mind would recommend that the long-stay patients be given the same medical treatment as the short-stay patients. Nor would any doctor recommend that all short-stay patients be diagnosed and treated in the same way, regardless of medical condition. Yet government bureaucrats ran the welfare state as if the recipients were all alike.

## PROBLEM NO. 5:
## CROWDING OUT THE PRIVATE SECTOR

Chances are that you have dropped some spare change into the Salvation Army tin at Christmas, donated to a school food drive, or helped out at a homeless soup kitchen. Private charities were helping out people long before government got in on the act, and they still offer the first tier of relief for those who have fallen on hard times. Yet the differences between the way welfare and private charities are run are very instructive.

Until recently, welfare was handed out to anyone who met a set of criteria. Applicants didn't have to explain how they'd come to be in their circumstances or give any indication of how they planned to brighten them in the future. They didn't even have to demonstrate a *desire* to improve their fortunes. In the AFDC program in most states, getting aid was a simple function of proving that you had: (1) low income, (2) very few assets, (3) dependent children, and (4) no man in the house. Anyone who satisfied these basic requirements was entitled to help. And the word "entitlement" was code for "right." Benefits could not be withdrawn simply because recipients refused to modify their behavior.

Private sector charities have always had a different and more enlightened philosophy. The best private charities do not believe that anyone has a "right" to their aid. Instead, they view charitable assistance as a tool that offers help, but also changes behavior. Most private charities vary the type of assistance they give from person to person. They also make it clear that they will reduce that help or take it away altogether if recipients don't demonstrate that they are attempting to set things right.

It's because of this different approach that private charities have been far more successful than entitlement programs at getting people back on their feet. And their success makes sense. Every person is different. Each needs assistance tailored to his or her needs. That's why private charities tend to practice hands-on management. They work with aid recipients to craft rehabilitation programs and they demand progress. Prior to welfare reform, that kind of support, counseling, and follow-up was virtually unheard of in federal welfare programs. When public welfare recipients requested counseling, they were usually passed along to private sector agencies.

Consider some of the other important differences between private work and entitlement programs. It's well known, for instance, that private sector charity is easy to get but hard to keep. Private charities work on the assumption that most people are fully capable of navigating life's twists and turns in the long run but that they may occasionally hit a pothole and need temporary help. Private sector agencies therefore make it very easy for applicants to obtain emergency relief and to obtain it quickly. It's only later that charities begin to demand proof of progress.

Government programs take the exact opposite approach. It's hard to get on welfare but easy to stay there. One study in the 1980s reported that in Texas the typical waiting period for food stamps was two to three weeks. It was even longer for AFDC, where applicants could spend a month waiting for aid after having filled out complicated and cumbersome forms. Some of the regulations were so complicated that the Dallas Salvation Army had to hire special staff to decipher them and be able to refer applicants to the right public agency.[16] Once these forms were mastered, however, aid recipients found that they could drift along in welfare for long periods of time.

Nationwide, of all the women who received welfare in any given year, some 60 percent received it the following one. Among women who received welfare for two consecutive years, about 70 percent received it a third year. And among those receiving welfare for four consecutive years, some 80 percent received it in the fifth year.[17]

A side effect of the spiraling up of government welfare spending is that it "crowds out" donations to private charities.[18] When government programs expand, private spending contracts. That's unfortunate, given how successful many of these charities are at getting people through crises. Even more so since it is private charities that are the real safety net in this country. Studies have found that the vast majority of low-income people, when faced with a real crisis, turn first to private agencies for help.[19] Churches, synagogues, and secular groups, for example, run 94 percent of all the shelters for the homeless in this country. Yet the expansion of the welfare state has meant less money is available for these front-line organizations.

## WELFARE REFORM

By the mid-1990s, the country had come to the end of its welfare tether. Americans realized that welfare as they knew it was no longer working and they demanded change. The federal government had taken some small steps in the early part of the decade by granting waivers that allowed state and local governments to experiment with reform. But the real triumph was in 1996, when Congress passed major legislation that extended reform to all the states.

What made the reform so important was that the government changed the very underpinnings of welfare, starting with the fact that it officially ended "welfare as a right." Federal funds were converted into block grants for state governments that were given broad authority to determine the terms and conditions of relief. And while states were given huge discretion, they were required to make adult welfare recipients go to work. They were also obliged to place a five-year lifetime limit on benefits. The only exceptions were for mothers with very young children.

In one fell swoop, America's welfare system went from "total entitlement" to "tough love." Even the new name of the program showed resolve. What had previously been called Aid to Families with Dependent Children was renamed *Temporary* Assistance for Needy Families (TANF). Critics (unsurprisingly) predicted disaster. When President Clinton signed the new legislation, three high level officials in his administration resigned in protest. An Urban Institute study predicted that an additional 1.1 million children would be thrown into poverty.[20] In the *New Republic*, Katha Pollitt wrote, "We know how welfare reform will turn out, too: wages will go down, families will fracture, millions of children will be more miserable than ever."[21]

As we reach the ten-year mark of reform, it's clear the critics were wrong. Welfare reform has been one of the most successful and inspiring public policy initiatives in the modern age. Between January 1994 and September 2000, almost three million families (representing 8.5 million people) left the welfare rolls. That was a drop of more than one out of two people on welfare. The number of families receiving aid has declined to a level that the country hasn't seen since the 1960s.[22]

Opponents of the change have suggested this drop in welfare roles was a function of a blossoming economy that created many new jobs, not reform. But June O'Neill, former head of the Congressional Budget Office, and Anne Hill at the City University of New York, conducted an exhaustive analysis of the drop and found this wasn't the case. More than half the decline in the welfare rolls, and more than 60 percent of the increase in employment among single mothers, was due to welfare reform. The researchers also found that less than one-fifth of this monumental societal progress in getting people off the dole could be attributed to an improving economy.[23]

Detractors also predicted that any drop in welfare rolls would come from skimming the cream off the top, putting only the "easy" cases back to work. Truly poor recipients, they worried, would stay stubbornly stuck in poverty and have few resources at their disposal. But this prediction also turned out to be wrong. If anything, the complete reverse has been true.

O'Neill and Hill found in the same study that the drop in welfare rolls was the largest for people who were classified as the most disadvantaged (see figure 11.2). They included young mothers (18 to 29 years old), mothers with children under the age of seven, high school dropouts, single black and Hispanic mothers, and women who had never been

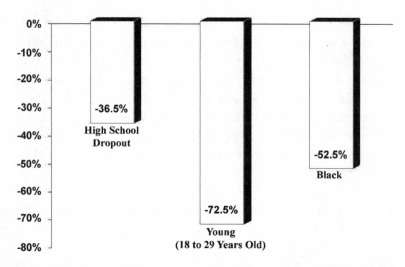

**FIGURE 11.2.** Percentage of Decline in Welfare Receipt by Disadvantaged Single Mothers Due to Welfare Reform, for the period 1996 to 2000. (Source: June E. O'Neill and M. Anne Hill, "Gaining Ground: Women, Welfare Reform and Work," National Center for Policy Analysis," NCPA Policy Report No. 251, February 2002.)

married. The biggest employment gains also went to the most "disadvantaged" single mothers (see figure 11.3). Welfare reform accounts for 40 percent of the increase in work participation among single mothers who are high school dropouts, 71 percent among 18- to 29-year-old single mothers, and 83 percent for black single mothers.[24]

## Building on Successful Reforms

By any measure, welfare reform has been an impressive achievement and something the country should take pride in having had the courage to implement. Yet there are still a number of improvements Congress can make to build on this success. These added reforms would both strengthen today's program and help ensure that the gains we've made so far don't unravel.

The Bush administration has proposed strengthening TANF work requirements while granting the states more flexibility in running the

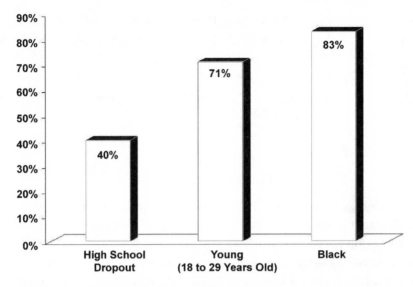

**FIGURE 11.3.** Percentage of Single Mothers' Employment Gains Attributed to Welfare Reform, for the period 1996 to 2000. (Source: June E. O'Neill and M. Anne Hill, "Gaining Ground: Women, Welfare Reform and Work," National Center for Policy Analysis," NCPA Policy Report No. 251, February 2002.)

programs.[25] The administration would require states to increase the amount of work required by recipients to 40 hours a week from the current 30 hours. At the same time, it would give states more flexibility in counting up to 16 hours of education, job training, and substance abuse treatment as part of the 40-hour requirement. Recipients would be able to receive benefits for three months during any two-year period while enrolled in substance abuse treatment.

The administration would also allow states to apply for waivers to federal rules covering other programs for the poor, such as food stamps, housing, workforce training, and adult education. History suggests that giving states this sort of flexibility is the best way to encourage smart reform. It was the states, after all, that really pioneered successful welfare reform by using waivers from federal AFDC regulations.

In all, the Bush administration has demonstrated a real commitment to making this reform work. Even though welfare rolls have declined by more than 50 percent, the administration has proposed maintaining the level of federal block grants to the states. If there is a threat, it comes from some welfare advocacy groups and members of Congress who would like to change the focus of TANF from work and independence to reducing "childhood poverty." In the past, "poverty reduction" has been code for increasing benefit checks. If there's one thing we've learned, it's that handing out greater amounts of money tends to encourage and prolong dependency.

## CHOICE IN CHARITY

Another high point of the 1996 welfare reform was that it recognized that faith-based charities play a crucial role in delivering social services via federally funded contracts or grants. The reform made it illegal to exclude organizations from receiving community service block grants and drug and alcohol treatment funds just because they were based on religion. It also prohibited federal agencies from controlling how these organizations express their beliefs or hire their staff.[26]

President Bush has since proposed expanding "charitable choice" to include other social service programs—a suggestion that has met with the usual wringing of hands and rending of garments. Some people are worried the federal money that goes to these groups might be used to promote religion. Others are concerned the regulations that already apply interfere too much with the charities' religious missions. We'd point out that there is a solution, a way to both unleash the power of religious social service providers while also keeping government away from the pulpit. It is called taxpayer choice.

## ENDING GOVERNMENT'S MONOPOLY

Before we get into taxpayer choice, let's first ask a basic question: Why should government dispense charity in the first place?

The traditional economic argument is that people will try to be "free riders" on the charitable giving of others. The theory works like this: Spending money to relieve poverty has social effects that extend beyond the interest of the giver. A person who buys a loaf of bread enjoys the full benefits of his purchase when he eats the loaf. Yet a gift to charity benefits not just the person who made the donation but everyone else in society who has an interest in the services the charity provides. As a result (or so goes the theory) individuals will tend to give too little. They will consider only their individual, private benefit from the gift and ignore the social benefits created for others. Given freedom of choice, people will tend to rely on others to make charitable gifts and fail to contribute their "fair share."

This argument has long been used to justify the government requirement that people give a certain portion of their incomes for the relief of poverty. It's an argument that, for the most part, people accept. But just because society has an obligation to provide a social safety net, it doesn't follow that government should nationalize the entire charity industry. Government requires drivers to carry automobile liability insurance, but few would argue that it is necessary or desirable for government to nationalize the auto liability insurance industry.

Nonetheless, government was becoming a public monopoly in the welfare industry. It was becoming the exclusive recipient of charitable contributions—taken by coercion, through the tax system—and usurping sole discretion over how these dollars are spent.

Like any monopoly that sets all the rules and operates under no competition, this government welfare system had become fat and lazy. Almost none of the welfare dollars ended up where givers wanted them to go. Private charity collects and disperses some $203 billion worth of gifts[27] because Americans trust that this money will be put to good purpose. Yet who ever heard of anyone voluntarily giving money to the TANF or food stamp programs? And when decisions about spending are at the mercy of the political process, it is the most powerful and organized special interests that have the most influence over where the money goes. It's no accident that more than two-thirds of federal welfare spending ends up in the pockets of people who are not poor.

The government can engage in wasteful, inefficient, and biased welfare practices because it has no fear of losing "contributors." Nor does it have to worry that it will lose its customers to groups that do a better job. The only way to remedy these defects is to denationalize public sector charity. Which brings us to taxpayer choice.

## TAXPAYER CHOICE

Imagine a local charity sent you literature asking for a donation for a new homeless shelter it was building. You like the idea and send off a check for $100. Not long afterward, you open your local paper to find that the charity had also been using some of the money it collected to build a plush new headquarters for the staff. You might be angry that your charitable donation had been used for this purpose and decide that next year you'll give to a different organization. That's your choice as a private donor. We need something equivalent in the public arena.

The basic idea of taxpayer choice is to allow individual taxpayers to choose how their "fair share" of money to the social safety net is spent. Government programs for the poor would compete with private charities for welfare tax dollars. When taxpayers donated to a qualified charity, they would be permitted to claim a credit on their federal income tax returns. Each dollar donated would reduce the taxpayer's tax liability by one dollar. The cost of the tax credits would be taken directly out of welfare block grants or matching fund payments to the states in which the taxpayer resides. In order to get their programs funded, states would have to prove to ordinary taxpayers that they could provide services as well as the private charities that are also asking for dollars.

The charities qualifying for tax credit–eligible donations would be those that provide relief and other services to the poor. Nonprofits with a broader mission, such as churches and colleges, could form subsidiaries for this purpose.[28] And since taxpayers have discretion over the money— money that is, after all, theirs to begin with—taxpayer choice should meet the same constitutional tests the U.S. Supreme Court has set up for public support of programs provided by religious institutions.[29]

Privatization of the welfare state through taxpayer choice would not only shift decisions about spending on the social safety net to individuals, it would fund those providers that can prove to taxpayers that they are truly helping people get back on their feet.

# NOTES

~

## CHAPTER 1

1. Claudia Goldin, *Understanding the Gender Gap: An Economic History of American Women* (New York: Oxford University Press, 1990), table 6.1, p. 162. When he was Speaker of the U.S. House of Representatives, Tip O'Neill supported many women's rights measures. But as Massachusetts Speaker of the House in 1950, he killed a bill that would have allowed newly married teachers to retain their jobs. See John Aloysius Farrell, *Tip O'Neill and the Democratic Century* (Boston: Little, Brown and Company, 2001), p. 114.

2. Lee Cullum, "This Texas Tornado Cleared A Path For Women's Progress," Opinion: Viewpoints, *Dallas Morning News*, July 2, 2003.

## CHAPTER 2

1. Cited in "Time Can Be More Important Than Money: Bring the Fair Labor Standards Act Into the 21st Century," Policy Backgrounder, Employment Policy Foundation, May 2, 2001, p. 1.

2. Current Population Survey, Household Data, Annual Averages, 2001. Table 8, "Employed and Unemployed Full- and Part-time Workers by Age, Sex, and Race."

3. Edward J. McCaffery, *Taxing Women: How the Marriage Penalty Affects Your Taxes* (Chicago: University of Chicago Press, 1997), pp. 142–44.

4. Sources: Employment Policy Foundation and the Bureau of Labor Statistics.

5. Department of Labor, Bureau of Labor Statistics, Current Population Survey, table 4. "Families with own children."

6. Reported in "Time Can Be More Important Than Money," p. 2.

7. James T. Bond, Ellen Galinsky, and Jennifer E. Swanberg, *The 1997 National Study of the Changing Workforce*, The Families and Work Institute, Pub. #W98-01,1998.

8. Employment Policy Foundation, "Changing Family Structure Demands Workplace Flexibility," April 4, 1997.

9. Center for Policy Alternatives Women's Program, "Women's Voices 2000," Key Findings.

10. Reported in "Time Can Be More Important Than Money," pp. 3–4.

11. See Denise Venable, "Labor Law Discriminates Against Women," National Center for Policy Analysis, NCPA Brief Analysis No. 365, August 6, 2001.

12. See U.S. Department of Labor, Bureau of Labor Statistics News, "Employer Costs for Employee Compensation Summary," March 18, 2003, http://www.bls.gov/news.release/ecec.nr0.htm. Wages and salaries in private industry averaged $17.06 per hour, with benefits adding an average $6.60.

13. "Tax Expenditures and Employee Benefits: An Update From the FY 2004 Budget," Facts from EBRI, Employee Benefits Research Institute, March 2003.

14. "Employee Benefits in Private Industry, 2000," U.S. Bureau of Labor Statistics, News USDL: 02-389, July 16, 2002.

15. In general, the unit cost of health insurance and retirement benefits is higher for small employers. See William J. Dennis, Jr., "Wages, Health Insurance and Pension Plans: the Relationship Between Employee Compensation and Small Business Owner Income," *Small Business Economics*, vol. 15, no. 4, December 2000, pp. 247–63.

16. Of persons working for businesses with fewer than 10 employees. See Paul Fronstin, "Sources of Health Insurance and Characteristics of the Uninsured: Analysis of the March 2003 Current Population Survey," Employee Benefit Research Institute, EBRI Issue Brief No. 264, December 2003, figure 10, p. 12.

17. Of persons working for businesses with fewer than 10 employees. Craig Copeland, "Employment-Based Retirement and Pension Plan Participation: Declining Levels and Geographic Differences," Employee Benefit Research Institute, EBRI Issue Brief No. 262, October 2003, figure 2, p. 7.

18. Diana Furchtgott-Roth and Christine Stolba, *Women's Figures: An Illustrated Guide to the Economic Progress of Women in America* (Washington, D.C.: The AEI Press and Independent Women's Forum, 1999).

19. The theory: If an employee can choose between taxable wages and an untaxed benefit, this amounts to "constructive receipt" of taxable income, even if the employee chooses the benefit. On this view, the benefit is regarded as equivalent to taxable income; therefore, it should be taxed as income. Based on

this reasoning, if an employer allows even one employee to choose between taxable wages and an untaxed benefit the employer risks making the benefits taxable to all other employees.

20. If the employer pays the woman more in wages when she forgoes health insurance coverage, the employer risks making the health insurance benefit taxable to all other employees. See the previous note.

21. See the discussion in McCaffery, *Taxing Women*, pp. 126–32.

22. See Alan B. Krueger and Bruce D. Meyer, "Labor Supply Effects of Social Insurance," NBER Working Paper No. w9014, June 2002; Gary Becker, "The Long-Term Unemployed Need Long-Term Help," 1991, reprinted in Gary S. Becker and Guity Nashat Becker, *The Economics of Life* (New York: McGraw-Hill, 1997); and the review in Raymond P. Thorne, "Paying People Not to Work: The Unemployment Compensation System," National Center for Policy Analysis, NCPA Policy Report No. 133, July 1988.

23. "Women, Low-Wage Workers and the Unemployment Compensation System: State Legislative Models for Change," revised edition, National Employment Law Project, October 1997, p. 1.

24. See "Part-Time Workers and Unemployment Insurance: Expanding UI for Low-Wage & Part-Time Workers," National Employment Law Project, revised February 2002, p. 1.

25. "Women, Low-Wage Workers," p. 3.

26. "Women, Low-Wage Workers," pp. 12–18.

27. "Women, Low-Wage Workers," pp. 3–4, 9.

28. See the proposal in Thorne, "Paying People Not to Work," pp. 29–31.

29. William B. Conerly, "Chile Leads the Way with Individual Unemployment Accounts," National Center for Policy Analysis, NCPA Brief Analysis No. 424, November 12, 2002.

30. At a minimum, for example, employers should be encouraged to pay high wages in lieu of health insurance for employees who can show proof of coverage under a spouse's plan.

## CHAPTER 3

1. Name has been changed.

2. "Work-Related Childcare Statistics," table I, Women's Bureau, U.S. Department of Labor, http://www.dol.gov/dol/wb/childcare/ccstats.htm, April 2000. While more than half of all mothers with children under the age of one are either working or looking for work, that number has fallen slightly over the

last three years, http://www.census.gov/population/socdemo/fertility/tabH5.pdf. See Stephanie Armous, "More Moms Make Kids their Career of Choice," *USA Today*, March 12, 2002.

3. Euston Quah, *The Economics of Home Production: Theory and Measurement* (Aldershot, U.K.: Ashgate, 1993) reviews 17 studies on household production and finds the international average estimate of household production is 34 percent of GNP. See also Joni Hersch, "The Economics of Home Production," *Southern California Review of Law and Women's Studies*, vol. 6, no. 2, Spring 1997, pp. 421–40; and Reuben Gronau, "The Theory of Home Production: The Past Ten Years," *Journal of Labor Economics*, vol. 15, no. 2, 1997.

4. In a survey of parents with children age five and under, only 6 percent thought that a quality childcare center was the best arrangement for young children. An impressive 70 percent thought the best arrangement is to have one parent at home and another 14 percent favored parents working in shifts so that one parent is always home. *Public Agenda*, June 2000, www.publicagenda.org.

5. Both the National Institutes of Health (NIH) and the U.S. Department of Health and Human Services (HHS) are conducting longitudinal studies that survey the effects of commercial childcare on children. One report in the ongoing study being conducted at NIH by the National Institute of Child Health and Human Development (NICHD) concluded that two- and three-year-olds evinced greater cognitive-linguistic functioning in high-quality childcare facilities than their peers in childcare arrangements not meeting recommended standards. See NICHD, "Results of NICHD Study of Early Childcare Reported at Society for Research in Child Development Meeting," April 3, 1997, http://www.nichd.nih.gov/new/releases/rel4top.cfm. On the other side, researchers also found that children in daycare are three times more likely to exhibit aggressive behavior (17 percent versus 5–6 percent) than children who stay with their parents. However, 83 percent of daycare children do not exhibit aggressive behavior and most of those who do are within the normal range. See NICHD, "Childcare Linked to Assertive, Noncompliant, and Aggressive Behaviors," NIH News, July 2003. See also Brian C. Robertson, *Day Care Deception: What the Childcare Establishment Isn't Telling Us* (San Francisco: Encounter Books, 2003), pp. 42–61.

6. A tax deduction for working mothers was first adopted in 1954, on the theory that such deductions were equivalent to business expenses. The law allowed a deduction of up to $600 of expenses and was phased out for families earning between $4,500 and $5,100. In 1976, the deduction was converted to a tax credit. The 1981 tax reform act raised both the ceiling on the credit and the percentage credit for lower-income families.

7. The Jobs Growth and Tax Relief Reconciliation Act of 2003 increased the Child Tax Credit from $600 to $1,000, but only for years 2003 and 2004. The full credit is available to married parents filing jointly if their adjusted gross income is less than $110,000 and to single parents who are heads of households if their income is less than $75,000. For purposes of the Child Tax Credit, the IRS defines a "qualifying child" as under age 17 at the end of 2003; a U.S. citizen; and claimed as a dependent. IRS, "Your Federal Income Tax: For Individuals," Publication 17.

8. See IRS, "Child and Dependent Care Expenses, for 2003," Publication 503. Several requirements must be met before expenses qualify for the DCTC. For example, filing status must be married filing jointly, single, head of household or qualifying widow(er) with dependent child; and the childcare service provider must be identified—if a commercial center, it must be certified, or if a nanny, must have payroll taxes paid. IRS, "Your Federal Income Tax: For Individuals," Publication 17.

9. Linda Giannarelli and James Barsimantov, "Childcare Expenses of America's Families" (Washington, D.C.: The Urban Institute, 2000), Occasional Paper No. 40, pp. 3–4. For those who pay for childcare services, their expenses constitute 9 percent of their families' earnings, likely the second largest expense in the family's budget after rent or mortgage.

10. Although the law applies to men as well as women, as a practical matter the law affects mainly the labor market activities of women. There have been a number of studies on the effects of subsidized daycare on female labor market participation. The President's Council of Economic Advisers reviewed the economics literature and concluded that "a 10% reduction in the price of childcare increases the probability a married mother will work by 2 to 8 percent." See "The Effects of Intervention," *The Economics of Childcare*, Council of Economic Advisers, December 1997, http://clinton3.nara.gov/wh/eop/cea/html/childcare.html. Childcare subsidies that reduce the price of childcare to low-income parents result in an increased employment rate for mothers with small children. Less-skilled women are more likely to base their decision to work on childcare subsidies. See David M. Blau, "Childcare Subsidy Programs," National Bureau of Economic Research, Working Paper w7806, July 2000; Patricia M. Anderson and Phillip B. Levine, "Childcare and Mothers' Employment Decisions," NBER Working Paper w7058, March 1999; David Blau and Erdal Tekin, "The Determinants and Consequences of Childcare Subsidies for Single Mothers," NBER Working Paper w9665, April 2003.

11. "1998 Individual Income Tax, All Returns: Tax Liabilities, Tax Credits, and Tax Payments, by Size of Adjusted Gross Income," *The Digital Daily*, IRS

Publication 1304, table 3.3, revised 4-2001, http://www.irs.ustreas.gov/pub/
irs-soi/98in33ar.xls. For earlier estimate, see David Henderson, "Childcare Tax
Credits: A Supply-Side Success Story," National Center for Policy Analysis, NCPA
Policy Report No. 140, July 1, 1989.

12. For more on arbitrary childcare tax relief, see the discussion in Alison P.
Hagy, "Childcare and Federal Tax Policy," *New York Law School Journal of Human
Rights*, vol. XVI, 1999, pp. 205–16.

13. The Dependent Care Spending Account and the Dependent Care Tax
Credit work in tandem for federal income tax purposes. When filing a tax
return, parents must subtract the amount of expenses reimbursed through their
spending accounts from the expenses used to calculate the DCTC.

14. Employers can depreciate the capital costs of childcare facilities and can
receive a tax credit of 25 percent of the expenses incurred in providing childcare services for their employees, but the credit cannot be more than $150,000
per year. In order to qualify, 80 percent of the children being cared for in the
facility must be employees' children.

15. "Work-Related Childcare Statistics," *Facts on Working Women Series*, U.S.
Department of Labor, Women's Bureau, July 2001.

16. See Jeffrey Capizzano, Gina Adams, and Freya Sonenstein, "Childcare
Arrangements for Children Under Five: Variation Across States," *New Federalism
National Survey of America's Families*, series B, no. B-7, The Urban Institute,
March 2000, pp. 1–3; and Linda Giannarelli and James Barsimantov, "Childcare
Expenses of America's Families," *Assessing the New Federalism*, Occasional Paper
No. 40, The Urban Institute, December 2000, pp. 3, 24.

17. In order to claim the Dependent Care Tax Credit, the taxpayer must identify the people and organizations that provide the care and provide their taxpayer identification. If the care provider comes to the home regularly, parents
must treat the person as a household employee, withholding Social Security
and Medicare taxes. If out-of-home providers care for more than six children,
they must comply with applicable state and local laws and regulations. To claim
the credit, in most cases then, the taxpayer must be using a business. IRS,
Publication 17.

18. See Capizzano, Adams, and Sonenstein, "Childcare Arrangements for
Children Under Five: Variation Across States," pp. 1–3; and Giannarelli and
Barsimantov, "Childcare Expenses of America's Families," pp. 3, 24.

19. Hagy, "Childcare and Federal Tax Policy," p. 212.

20. Virginia Postrel, "Who's Behind the Day-Care Crisis?" *Reason*, June 1989,
p. 25.

21. Joanne H. Pratt, *Homebased Business: The Hidden Economy*, Joanne H. Pratt Associate, Office of Advocacy, U.S. Small Business Administration, August 1999, pp. ESi–ESv.

22. Luisa Kroll, "Entrepreneur Moms," *Forbes Magazine*, May 18, 1998.

23. Joanne Pratt, "Legal Barriers to Home-Based Work," National Center for Policy Analysis, NCPA Policy Report No. 129, September 1987.

24. Some of these restrictions were successfully contested. See Postrel, "Who's Behind the Day-Care Crisis?"

25. Robertson, *Day Care Deception*, pp. 92–121.

26. Postrel, "Who's Behind the Day-Care Crisis?" p. 24.

27. Henderson, "Childcare Tax Credit." For an extensive analysis of the harmful effects of occupational licensing regulations, see Milton Friedman, *Capitalism and Freedom* (Chicago: University of Chicago Press, 1961); S. David Young, *The Role of Experts: Occupational Licensing in America* (Washington, D.C.: Cato Institute, 1987); and John Goodman, *Regulation of Medical Care: Is the Price Too High?* (Washington, D.C.: Cato Institute, 1980).

## CHAPTER 4

This chapter is partly based on Edward J. McCaffery, *Taxing Women*, pbk. ed. (Chicago: University of Chicago Press, 1999); and McCaffery, "Women and Taxes," National Center for Policy Analysis, NCPA Policy Report No. 250, February 2002.

1. For an economic analysis of the marriage penalty, including a description of its historical development, see Bruce Bartlett, "The Marriage Penalty," National Center for Policy Analysis, NCPA Policy Backgrounder No. 145, February 9, 1998.

2. Income tax brackets and rates as reflected in the 2003 tax legislation. See www.cch.com.

3. In this particular discussion, we are assuming it is the wife who is the secondary earner and is pushed into a higher tax bracket by her higher-earning husband. However, in about 20 to 25 percent of dual-earner couples, the wife earns more than the husband. Interestingly, there are considerable differences among families when arrayed by total income. Among the lowest one-fifth by family income, 55 percent of the wives make more than their husbands. Among the highest one-fifth, only 6 percent of wives earn more than their husbands. See Edward J. McCaffery, *Taxing Women* (Chicago: The University of Chicago Press, 1997).

4. "Does It Pay Both Spouses To Work?" National Center for Policy Analysis, NCPA Policy Report No. 260, May 2003, pp. 6–9.

5. For a discussion of how a flat tax might work, see Robert E. Hall and Alvin Rabushka, *Low Tax, Simple Tax, Flat Tax* (New York: McGraw-Hill, 1983).

6. For a discussion of how a national sales tax might work, see Laurence J. Kotlikoff, "The Economic Impact of Replacing Federal Income Taxes With a Sales Tax," Cato Institute, Cato Policy Analysis No. 193, April 15, 1993.

7. Married couples can file as "married filing separately," but this does not give them the same benefit as true, independent filing.

## CHAPTER 5

1. The Consolidated Omnibus Budget Reconciliation Act (COBRA) allows departed employees the right to continue the group benefits provided by their former employer's insurance plan for a limited time. They may, however, be required to pay up to 102 percent of the cost of the plan.

2. John C. Goodman and Gerald L. Musgrave, "Twenty Myths About National Health Insurance," National Center for Policy Analysis, NCPA Policy Report No. 128, December 1991. For an account of rationing by waiting in Canada, see Michael Walker and Greg Wilson, "Waiting Your Turn: Hospital Waiting Lists in Canada," 11th edition, Fraser Institute, Critical Issues Bulletin, September 2001. For an analysis of the effects of rationing in Britain's National Health Service, see David Green and Laura Casper, *Delay, Denial, and Dilution: The Impact of NHS Rationing on Heart Disease and Cancer* (London: Institute of Economic Affairs, 2000).

3. Klea D. Bertakis, Rahman Aeari, Edward J. Callahan, L. Jay Helms, and John A. Robbins, "Gender Differences in the Utilization of Health Care Services," *Journal of Family Practice*, vol. 49, no. 2, February 2000.

4. Wye River Group on Healthcare, Public Opinion Polling: Past and Present, May 2002.

5. Bertakis, Azari, Helms, Callahan, and Robbins, "Gender Differences in the Utilization of Health Care Services," pp. 147–52.

6. *Kaiser Women's Health Survey*, Kaiser Family Foundation, May 2002. The findings are the result of a telephone survey conducted of 3,966 women, ages 18 to 64, in the United States in the spring and summer of 2001. A companion survey was conducted of 700 men for gender comparisons.

7. Of women aged 18–64, 27 percent get coverage through "dependent or family coverage," 34 percent get it from own job, 19 percent are uninsured, 9 percent are on Medicaid, 6 percent have individual coverage, and 5 percent

have coverage of unknown origins. Citation, Alina Salganicoff et al., "Women's Health in the United States: Health Coverage and Access to Care," *Kaiser Women's Health Survey*, p. 13, figure 7.

8. For a discussion of women's workforce behavior see Diana Furchtgott-Roth and Christine Stolba, *Women's Figures: An Illustrated Guide to the Economic Progress of Women in America* (Washington, D.C.: The AEI Press and Independent Women's Forum, 1999).

9. Kaiser Health Poll Report, November/December 2002. According to the Kaiser reports on health security since 1999, 15 percent more women than men report being concerned about health care.

10. "Employer Costs for Employee Compensation—September 2002," Bureau of Labor Statistics, U.S. Department of Labor, December 11, 2002; The Kaiser Family Foundation and Health Research and Educational Trust, "Employer Health Benefits: 2002 Annual Survey," Report No. 3251, Kaiser Family Foundation, September 2002.

11. Sally Trude, "Who Has a Choice of Health Plans?" *Center for Studying Health System Change*, Issue Brief No. 27, February 2000.

12. Atul A. Gawande et al., "Does Dissatisfaction With Health Plans Stem From Having No Choices?" *Health Affairs*, vol. 17, no. 5, September/October 1998, pp. 184–94.

13. Seventy-five percent of women rate the benefits offered as very important in determining their choice and 57 percent rate the plan's doctors as very important. See *Kaiser Women's Health Survey*, May 2002.

14. David O. Weber, "Health herstory—a compendium of resources," *Healthcare Forum Journal*, vol. 37, no. 1, Jan–Feb 1994, pp. 37–51.

15. John D. Graham, "Comparing Opportunities To Reduce Health Risks: Toxin Control, Medicine and Injury Prevention," National Center for Policy Analysis, NCPA Policy Report No. 192, June 1995.

16. See "Is Preventive Medical Care Cost-Effective?" National Center for Policy Analysis, Brief Analysis No. 188, November 9, 1995. The Office of Technology Assessment (OTA) studied the cost-effectiveness of adding coverage for several preventive measures—including flu and pneumonia vaccines and screening tests for cervical and colon cancer—to the federal Medicare insurance program for the elderly. *None of the preventive measures was found to cut costs.* See U.S. Congress, Office of Technology Assessment, *Preventive Health Services for Medicare Beneficiaries: Policy and Research Issues* (Washington, D.C.: U.S. Government Printing Office, February 1990); and U.S. Congress, Office of Technology Assessment, *The Cost and Electiveness of Colorectal Screening in the Elderly—Background Paper* (Washington, D.C.: U.S. Government Printing

Office, September 1990). A separate study by the OTA found that only three kinds of preventive care save money: prenatal care for poor women, tests in newborns for certain congenital disorders, and most childhood immunizations. See U.S. Congress, Office of Technology Assessment, *Benefit Design in Health Care Reform: Report #1—Clinical Preventive Services* (Washington, D.C.: U.S. Government Printing Office, September 1993).

17. Graham, "Comparing Opportunities To Reduce Health Risks: Toxin Control, Medicine and Injury Prevention."

18. A review of the literature called into question all past studies that affirmed the value of mammograms. Ole Olsen and Peter C. Gøtzsche, "Cochrane Review on Screening for Breast Cancer with Mammography," *Lancet*, vol. 358, no. 9290, October 20, 2001. For an explanation of the issues for lay readers, see Barron H. Lerner, "What's Behind It All," *Washington Post*, March 1, 2002.

19. Susan S. Laudicina, Betsy Losleben, and Natasha Walker, "State Legislative Health Care and Insurance Issues: 2001 Survey of Plans," Blue Cross and Blue Shield Association, December 2001.

20. Jan Ziegler, "The Gender Gap: Health Care's Next Frontier," *Business and Health*, vol. 16, no. 11, November 1998.

21. Weber, "Health: Herstory."

22. John C. Goodman, "MSAs for Everyone, Part III," National Center For Policy Analysis, Brief Analysis No. 356, April 19, 2001.

23. Greg Scandlen, "Medical Savings Accounts: Obstacles to Their Growth and Ways to Improve Them," National Center For Policy Analysis, NCPA Policy Report No. 216, July 1998.

24. Greg Scandlen, "MSAs for Everyone, Part II," National Center For Policy Analysis, Brief Analysis No. 319, March 31, 2000.

25. About 80 percent of South Africans rely on the country's "free" public health system. See Shaun Matisonn, "Medical Savings Accounts in South Africa," National Center For Policy Analysis, NCPA Policy Report No. 234, June 2000.

26. Michael F. Cannon, "Three Avenues to Patient Power," National Center for Policy Analysis, Brief Analysis No. 430, January 30, 2003.

27. For instance, a taxpayer in the 25 percent bracket with 15.3 percent FICA tax and 5 percent state income tax is getting a 45.3 percent subsidy.

28. Unlike employer-sponsored health insurance, premiums paid by the self-employed do not escape the 15.3 percent payroll tax.

29. Federal law allows all taxpayers to deduct health (and health insurance) expenses above 7.5 percent of adjusted gross incomes.

30. John Sheils, Paul Hogan, and Randall Haught, "Health Insurance and Taxes: The Impact of Proposed Changes in Current Federal Policy," National Coalition on Health Care, October 18, 1999.

31. For a discussion on reasons for government intervention in health care, see James M. Poterba, "Government Intervention in the Markets for Education and Health Care: How and Why?" in Victor R. Fuchs, ed., *Individual and Social Responsibility: Childcare, Education, Medical Care, and Long-term Care in America* (Chicago: University of Chicago Press, 1996), pp. 277–304. However, the real reasons for government intervention in health insurance markets are likely to be political. See Veronique deRugy and Tom Miller, "An Asymmetric Bias toward Government Regulation," *Health Care News*, December 2001.

32. Just 5 percent (7.3 million) of those offered employer-sponsored coverage decline and remain uninsured, representing 20 percent of all those without insurance. See Peter J. Cunningham, Elizabeth Schaefer, and Christopher Hogan, "Who Declines Employer-Sponsored Health Insurance and Is Uninsured?" Center for Studying Health System Change, Issue Brief No. 22, October 1999.

33. See Devon M. Herrick, "Uninsured by Choice," National Center for Policy Analysis, Brief Analysis No. 379, November 15, 2001; and Naomi Lopez Bauman and Devon M. Herrick, "Uninsured in the Lone Star State," National Center for Policy Analysis, Brief Analysis No. 335, Tuesday, August 29, 2000.

34. However, women are 20 percent more likely to face access barriers—especially if they're uninsured. See Jeanne M. Lambrew, "Diagnosing Disparities in Health Insurance for Women: A Prescription for Change," *Commonwealth Fund*, August 2001. http://www.cmwf.org/usr_doc/lambrew_disparities_493.pdf.

35. Carole Keeton Rylander, Texas Comptroller of Public Accounts, "Texas Estimated Health Care Spending on the Uninsured," May 9, 2000. The Comptroller's office estimates that $4.7 billion was spent on the uninsured in fiscal 1998. Of this amount approximately $890 million consisted of unreimbursed physician services.

36. Jack Hadley and John Holahan, "How Much Medical Care Do the Uninsured Use, and Who Pays for It?" *Health Affairs*, Web exclusive, February 12, 2003.

37. Peter J. Cunningham and Michael H. Park, "Recent Trends in Children's Health Insurance: No Gains for Low-Income Children," Center for Studying Health System Change, Issue Brief No. 29, April 2000; and "Health Care Coverage," Children Trends Databank, www.childtrendsdatabank.org/indicators/26HealthCareCoverage.cfm.

38. Devon M. Herrick, "Uninsured by Choice."

39. Karen M. Beauregard, "Persons Denied Private Health Insurance Due To Poor Health," Agency for Health Care Policy and Research, Report No. 92-0016, December 1991.

40. Melinda L. Schriver and Grace-Marie Arnett, "Uninsured Rates Rise Dramatically In States With Strictest Health Insurance Regulations," Heritage Foundation, Backgrounder No. 1211, August 14, 1998.

41. Len M. Nichols, "Health Care Quality: At What Cost?" The Urban Institute, no. 13, May 1998.

42. See Randall R. Bovbjerg, Alison Evans Cuellar, and John Holahan, "Market Competition and Uncompensated Care Pools," Urban Institute, Occasional Paper Number 35, March 2000; and David Blumenthal, "Briefing Note: Indigent Care: A Shared Responsibility," The Commonwealth Fund, April 2001.

43. Bauman and Herrick, "Uninsured in the Lone Star State."

44. See John C. Goodman, "Two Cheers for the Bush Health Plan," National Center for Policy Analysis, NCPA Brief Analysis No. 398, February 19, 2001.

45. See, for example, John C. Goodman, "Characteristics of an Ideal Health Care System," National Center for Policy Analysis, NCPA Policy Report No. 242, April 2002; John C. Goodman, "Reforming the U.S. Health Care System," National Center for Policy Analysis, NCPA Backgrounder No. 149, April 26, 1999; Thomas R. Saving and Andrew J. Rettenmaier, "Saving Medicare," National Center For Policy Analysis, NCPA Policy Report No. 222, January 1999; and Greg Scandlen, "Defined Contribution Health Insurance," National Center For Policy Analysis, Policy Backgrounder No. 154, October 26, 2000.

## CHAPTER 6

1. *A Nation at Risk: The Imperative for Educational Reform*, The National Commission on Excellence in Education, April 1983, http//www.ed.gov/pubs/NatAtRisk/.

2. Andrew Rettenmaier and Donald R. Deere, "Economic Mobility," National Center for Policy Analysis and Financial Services Roundtable, Brief Analysis No. 449, July 23, 2003.

3. Employment Policy Foundation, "EPF Employment Snapshot: July 2003," www.epf.org.

4. Among the many histories that track education reform efforts, the most comprehensive is Diane Ravitch, *Left Back: A Century of Failed School Reforms* (New York: Simon & Schuster, 2000).

5. The unionization of the National Education Association (NEA) in the 1960s forever altered education governance. See Charlene K. Haar, *The Politics of the PTA* (New Brunswick, N.J.: Transaction Publishers, 2002), pp. 76–84.

6. These results are not only broken down by school but also by race and ethnic origin. The public is now able to see the alarming gap between African-American or Latino students and white or Asian-American students. According to Abigail Thernstrom and Stephan Thernstrom, "By twelfth grade, on average, black students are four years behind those who are white or Asian. Hispanics don't do much better." *No Excuses: Closing the Racial Gap in Learning* (New York: Simon & Schuster, 2003), p. 12.

7. This section is largely based on John C. Goodman and Matt Moore, "School Choice vs. School Choice," National Center for Policy Analysis, NCPA Backgrounder No. 155, April 27, 2001.

8. See Shawna Grosskopf, Kathy Hayes, Lori Taylor, and William Webber, "Allocative Inefficiency and School Competition," Federal Reserve Bank of Dallas Working Paper #97-08, 1997.

9. That premium may be a bargain if it is compared to the present value of 12 years of tuition at an expensive private school.

10. *The Two-Income Trap: Why Middle-Class Mothers & Fathers are Going Broke* (New York: Basic Books, 2003), pp. 22–32.

11. In a recent survey by the National Center for Education Statistics, 16 states reported having magnet schools—although not all states responded. Those with the most magnet schools were California (472 schools with 9.3 percent of the state's student body), Illinois (315 schools and 11.6 percent of the student body), and North Carolina (119 schools and 6.1 percent of the student body). See "Overview of Public Elementary and Secondary Schools and Districts: School Year 1998–1999," National Center for Education Statistics, Statistics in Brief, June 2000, http://nces.ed.gov/pubs2000/2000333.pdf.

12. Most large city school districts are (or have been) under federal court order for decades. This means that all schools—magnet schools as well as other schools—already have been under the control of federal judges for some time.

13. A recent report by the State University of New York shows that District 4 continues to have widespread improvement in math and reading test scores compared with the other districts in the city. See Robert E. Moffit, Jennifer Garrett, and Janice A. Smith, eds., "School Choice 2001: What's Happening in the States," The Heritage Foundation, 2001, p. 158.

14. Since virtually any private school can become a charter school, in effect Arizona's charter school system is a thinly disguised voucher system.

15. Lewis Solomon and Mary Gifford, "Teacher Accountability in Charter Schools," National Center for Policy Analysis and CEO America, Brief Analysis No. 285, March 1, 1999.

16. Virginia Walden, "The Case for School Choice in Washington, D.C.," in John C. Goodman and Fritz E. Steiger, eds., *An Education Agenda: Let Parents Choose Their Children's School* (Dallas, Tex.: National Center for Policy Analysis, 2001), p. 98.

17. Mac Fisher, "To Each His Own," *The Washington Post*, April 8, 2001, p. W28.

18. Janet R. Beales and Thomas F. Bertonneau, "Do Private Schools Serve Difficult-to-Educate Students?" Mackinac Center for Public Policy and the Reason Foundation, October 1997.

19. See the review in Goodman and Moore, "School Choice vs. School Choice."

20. Almost all industrialized nations allow school choice. According to a study of school systems in two dozen countries, "Public funding is provided in virtually every country . . . to allow parents to send their children to whatever school they choose." Charles Glenn and Jan de Groof, "Last Holdout Against Educational Freedom," *The American Enterprise*, April/May 2003, p. 36.

21. National Center for Education Statistics, "Homeschooling in the United States: 1999," U.S. Department of Education, July 2001, NCES 2001-33.

22. Per pupil expenditures rose 58 percent in real terms during the 1960s, 27 percent in the 1970s, and 29 percent during the 1980s and 1990s. In dollar terms, average real spending per pupil in public schools climbed from just under $2,000 to just over $6,000 from 1960 to 1996. At the same time, the number of pupils per teacher declined from 26 to 17 and salaries for instructional staff increased from $25,206 to $39,451. However, despite the additional resources, test scores remained stagnant or declined. Academic studies consistently find that there is no clear relationship between school expenditures and student performance. See Eric A. Hanushek, Steven G. Rivkin, and Lori L. Taylor, "Aggregation and the Estimated Effects of School Resources," *Review of Economics and Statistics*, vol. 78, no. 4, November 1996, pp. 611–27.

23. Paul Ciotti, "Money and School Performance: Lessons from the Kansas City Desegregation Experiment," Cato Institute Policy Analysis No. 298, March 16, 1998.

24. "Prospects: The Congressionally Mandated Study of Educational Growth and Opportunity," U.S. Department of Education, 1997, http://www.ed.gov/offices/OUS/PES/esed/prospect.html.

25. Nina S. Rees, "Public School Benefits of Private School Vouchers," *Policy Review*, no. 93, January–February 1999.

26. Susan Lee and Christine Foster, "Trustbusters," *Forbes*, June 2, 1997, pp. 146–52.

27. Howard Fuller, Introduction to Carol Innerst, "Competing to Win: How Florida's A+ Plan Has Triggered Public School Reform," Center for Education Reform, Washington, D.C., April 2000, http://edreform.com/school_choice/compete.htm.

28. Department of Education, "What to Know & Where to Go: Parents' Guide to *No Child Left Behind*," April 2002, p. 20.

29. National Center for Education Statistics, "Academic Background of College Graduates Who Enter and Leave Teaching" Indicator 31, p. 91. An even more dismal finding is that graduates who scored in the bottom quartile were more likely to have taught in public elementary schools where 50 percent or more of the children were eligible for free or reduced-price lunches.

30. Peter Brimelow, *The Worm in the Apple: How the Teacher Unions Are Destroying American Education* (New York: HarperCollins Publishers, 2003), pp. 225–27.

31. "Where the NEA Pulls the Strings," *The Washington Times*, November 14, 2002, A22. The NEA and AFT together contributed more than $2.5 million to Democratic congressional candidates by October 2002. Robert Holland reports that NEA spends one-third ($90 million) of its annual income on political activities in "Teacher Unions Promote a Political Agenda," *School Reform News*, July 1, 2003.

32. Caroline Hoxby, "Would School Choice Change the Teaching Profession?" National Bureau of Economic Research, Working Paper 7866, August 2000, pp. 34–36.

33. U.S. Department of Education, "Meeting the Highly Qualified Teachers Challenge: The Secretary's Second Annual Report on Teacher Quality," 2003, pp. 7–24.

## CHAPTER 7

1. B. Douglas Bernheim, Jonathan Skinner, and Steven Weinberg, "What Accounts for the Variation in Retirement Wealth Among U.S. Households?" National Bureau of Economic Research, Working Paper No. W6227, October 1997, http://papers.nber.org/papers/W6227.

2. See Patrick J. Purcell, "Retirement Savings and Household Wealth: A Summary of Recent Data," Congressional Research Service, December 11, 2003.

3. Purcell, "Retirement Savings and Household Wealth."

4. See Vickie Bajtelsmit, Alexandra Bernasek, and Nancy Jianakoplos, "Gender Differences in Defined Contribution Pension Decisions," *Financial Services Review*, vol. 8, 1999, p. 5.

5. Vickie Bajtelsmit, "Women as Retirees," *Women's Agenda: Ideas to Reform Institutions*, National Center for Policy Analysis, March 2002, pp. 75–98.

6. C. Eugene Steuerle, "Divorce and Social Security," National Center for Policy Analysis, NCPA Brief Analysis No. 291, May 21, 1999.

7. Internal Revenue Service, publication 590, "Individual Retirement Arrangements." The contribution limit gradually increases to $5,000 in 2008 when it is indexed to inflation.

8. The amount of tax deduction is subject to income limitations if both spouses are covered by a work retirement plan. For a spouse filing a joint return, the limit on Adjusted Gross Income (AGI) is $70,000. For a spouse filing separately, the AGI limit is $10,000.

9. Martin Feldstein, "The Effects of Tax-Based Saving Incentives on Government Revenue and National Saving," NBER Working Paper No. 4021, March 1992, National Bureau of Economic Research; and R. Glenn Hubbard and Jonathan S. Skinner, "Assessing the Effectiveness of Saving Incentives," NBER Working Paper No. 5686, July 1996, National Bureau of Economic Analysis. These and other studies show that decreased government revenues would be made up with expanded investments in the domestic economy.

10. Steven F. Venti and David A. Wise, "Aging and Housing Equity: Another Look," NBER Working Paper No. 8608, November 2001. Rarely do retirees cash out of their home equity to finance retirement; instead, most use the asset as a reserve for catastrophic circumstances.

11. Survey conducted by the Luntz Research Companies/Mark A. Siegel and Associates for Third Millennium, September 1994, http://www.thirdmil.org/publications/surveys/surv7.html.

12. The www.mysocialsecurity.org Web site is sponsored by NCPA. Here you may calculate your own Social Security benefit based on your age and earnings.

13. See the discussion of this and other examples in Edward J. Harpham, "Private Pensions in Crisis: The Case for Radical Reform," National Center for Policy Analysis, NCPA Policy Report No. 115, January 1984.

14. The law was the Employee Retirement Income Security Act (ERISA) of 1974.

15. The existence of federal pension insurance does not guarantee all pension promises will be kept, however. The reason is that the PBGC sets a maximum on the amount it will pay to each retiree. For example, after Braniff filed for bankruptcy in 1982, retired teamsters receiving monthly pension checks of

$665 saw their benefits reduced to $434. Retired machinists saw their monthly pension checks cut from $700 to $590. Harding Lawrence, former CEO of Braniff, had been counting on a $306,000-a-year pension. Under the bail-out, his pension was reduced to $16,568 a year. See Harpham, "Private Pensions in Crisis," p. 7.

16. However, at the time ERISA was passed it is doubtful that Congress antic- ipated the explosive growth of 401(k) plans. If they had, some member would have proudly put his or her name on it (like the Roth IRA) rather than have it described by the numerical section of the law. This is why Department of Labor analyst Richard Hinz calls the 401(k) the "accidental pension." See "A Matter of Definition," *The Economist*, February 16, 2002, p. 3.

17. The counterpart of the 401(k) for nonprofit organizations, including col- leges and universities, is the 403(b) plan. Employers may also establish a Savings Incentive Match Plan for Employees (SIMPLE). Self-employed individuals can take advantage of a Simplified Employee Pension (SEP) plan, or a Keogh Profit Sharing plan. According to some analysts, the new tax law also allows the self- employed to set up a "one-person 401(k) plan." See Karen Damato, "The One- Man Band Gets a 401(k) Gift: A Lucky Benefit For the Self-Employed," *Wall Street Journal*, August 17, 2001.

18. Withdrawals without penalty may be made at age 59½. Other than "hard- ship" withdrawals approved by an employer, withdrawals before age 59½ are subject to a 15 percent penalty on top of normal income taxes.

19. Unless the employee is over 50, then she may take advantage of a "catch- up" provision that allows her to shelter $14,000 for 2003.

20. More than 48 million workers have accumulated more than $1.8 trillion in defined-contribution plans. See Abstract of 1997 Form 5500 Annual Reports, U.S. Department of Labor, Pension and Welfare Benefits Administration, "Private Pension Plan Bulletin," no. 10, Winter 2001.

21. "A Matter of Definition."

22. Bajtelsmit, "Women as Retirees."

23. K. Ferguson and K. Blackwell, *The Pension Book: What You Need to Know to Prepare for Retirement* (New York: Arcade Publishing, 1995), pp. 37–47.

24. Employer plus employee total annual contributions to a defined-contri- bution plan like a 401(k) or 403(b) is limited to $40,000 per year, or 25 percent of the employee's compensation, whichever is less. The Economic Growth and Tax Relief Reconciliation Act of 2001 raised the previous $30,000 limit to $40,000 in 2002.

25. Employee contributions to 401(k)s, 403(b)s, and other tax-deferred accounts is limited to $12,000 in 2003. The Economic Growth and Tax Relief

Reconciliation Act of 2001 incrementally raises the maximum annual individual contribution by $1,000 per year to $15,000 by 2007.

26. Individuals under age 50 who are not participating in an employer-sponsored plan can only contribute $3,000 to an IRA in 2003. The Economic Growth and Tax Relief Reconciliation Act of 2001 incrementally raises the maximum contribution to $5,000 by 2008. While this limit will increase under current law, it is still only about half of the contribution allowed to an employer-sponsored plan.

27. Vickie L. Bajtelsmit and Alexandra Bernasek, "Why Do Women Invest Differently Than Men?" *Financial Counseling and Planning*, vol. 7, 1996, pp. 5–6.

28. Bajtelsmit, "Women as Retirees."

29. "Investment Relations: Defined-Benefits vs. 401(k)," *Watson Wyatt Insider*, September 1998.

30. Brooks Hamilton and Scott Burns, "Reinventing Retirement Income," National Center for Policy Analysis, NCPA Policy Report No. 248, December 2001.

31. Hamilton and Burns, "Reinventing Retirement Income."

32. Brooks Hamilton, "Learning Our Lesson from Enron," *Washington Times*, February 2, 2002.

33. Hamilton and Burns, "Reinventing Retirement Income," p. 12.

34. For example, Vickie L. Bajtelsmit, "Conservative Pension Investing: How Much Difference Does It Make?" *Benefits Quarterly*, vol. 12, no. 2, 1996, pp. 35–39.

35. See the review of the literature in Bajtelsmit and Bernasek, "Why Do Women Invest Differently Than Men?" pp. 1–10; and in Bajtelsmit, "Women as Retirees."

36. Brad Barber and Terrance Odean, "Trading is Hazardous to Your Wealth: The Common Stock Investment Performance of Individual Investors," *Journal of Finance*, vol. LV, no. 2, April 2000, pp. 773–806, http//faculty.haas.berkeley.edu/odean/papers/returns/returns.html.

37. Hal R. Varian, "Economic Scene: Investor Behavior Clouds the Wisdom of Offering Wider Choice in 401(k)s," *New York Times*, February 14, 2002.

38. Hamilton and Burns, "Reinventing Retirement Income," p. 13.

39. Only about a third of large, multisite corporations who are members of the Profit Sharing Council of America give investment counseling to employees, usually through online resources. Half of all members provide such advice, up from 35.2 percent in 2000. Source: David Wray, president, Profit Sharing Council of America.

40. See, for example, Scott Burns, "Go Index Funds for the Long Term," *Dallas Morning News*, February 12, 2002.

41. See the discussion in Hamilton and Burns, "Reinventing Retirement Income," pp. 17–19. Hamilton and Burns would also discourage preretirement, lump sum distributions. A 1988 *Current Population Survey* found that women were 40 percent more likely than men to receive such a payment. Only half of each group rolled the payment over into another savings or retirement plan. See also Bajtelsmit and Berask, "Why Do Women Invest Differently Than Men?" p. 5.

42. Jagadeesh Gokhale and Laurence J. Kotlikoff, "Tax-Favored Savings Accounts: Who Gains? Who Loses?" National Center for Policy Analysis, NCPA Policy Report No. 249, January 2002.

43. For the explanation of the Social Security benefits tax and how it affects marginal tax rates, see Stephen J. Entin, "Reducing the Social Security Benefits Tax," National Center for Policy Analysis, NCPA Brief Analysis No. 332, August 2000.

44. Gokhale and Kotlikoff, "Tax-Favored Savings Accounts."

## CHAPTER 8

1. When collecting benefits before full retirement age, $1 in benefits is deducted for every $2 earned above the annual limit ($11,640 for 2004) and $1 for every $3 earned above a higher annual limit ($31,080 for 2004). These earnings limit penalties are dropped once the beneficiary reaches full retirement age.

2. See C. Rudolph Penner, "Women and Social Security," *Women's Agenda: Ideas to Reform Institution*, National Center for Policy Analysis, March 2002, pp. 99–126.

3. The 2001 Annual Report of the Boards of Trustees of the Federal Old-Age and Survivors Insurance and Disability Insurance Trust Funds, table V, A3.

4. Calculations by Andy Rettenmaier, Texas A&M University. For an explanation of the model that produces these results, see Liqun Lin and Andrew J. Rettenmaier, "Comparing Proposals for Social Security Reform," National Center for Policy Analysis, NCPA Policy Report No. 227, September 1999, appendix A.

5. Calculations by Andy Rettenmaier, Texas A&M University.

6. Alice Kessler-Harris, "Designing Women and Old Fools: The Construction of the Social Security Amendments of 1939," *U.S. History As Women's History* (Chapel Hill: University of North Carolina Press, 1995), p. 100.

7. Vickie Bajtelsmit, "Women as Retirees," *Women's Agenda: Ideas to Reform Institutions*, National Center for Policy Analysis, March 2002, pp. 75–98.

8. Rochelle Stanfield and Corinna Nicolaou, "Social Security: Out of Step with the Modern Family," Urban Institute, April 2000.

9. C. Eugene Steuerle, "Divorce and Social Security," National Center for Policy Analysis, NCPA Brief Analysis No. 291, May 21, 1999.

10. There is a family maximum benefit, which is generally equal to 150 to 180 percent of the earner's retirement benefit in 2002.

11. Unmarried children under age 18 (or up to age 19 if attending elementary or secondary school full-time) are eligible for Social Security survivor's benefits. Children may also receive benefits at any age if the child was disabled before age 22 and remained disabled.

12. C. Eugene Steuerle, "Divorce and Social Security," National Center for Policy Analysis, Brief Analysis No. 291, May 1999.

13. Under the income tax law, for example, the (secondary earner) wife is taxed at her husband's marginal tax rate. However, the Social Security payroll tax ignores the husband's payroll taxes (and the wife's right to benefits based on those taxes) in imposing a tax on the wife.

14. See C. Eugene Steuerle and Jon M. Bakija, *Retooling Social Security for the 21st Century* (Washington, D.C.: Urban Institute, 1994) pp. 213–14.

15. John C. Goodman, "Social Security Reform: The NCPA's Hybrid Plan," National Center for Policy Analysis, NCPA Brief Analysis No. 385, December 18, 2001.

## CHAPTER 9

1. The unlimited federal estate tax marital deduction that allows the surviving spouse to inherit all common property became law with the passage of the Economic Recovery Tax Act of 1981. Before ERTA, transfer of property to a surviving spouse was governed by a host of complicated rules. See Robert A. Esperti and Renno L. Peterson, *Protect Your Estate*, 2nd ed. (New York: McGraw-Hill, 2000), pp. 63–66.

2. Estate taxes are usually due nine months after the decedent's death. When the estate is not liquid, survivors are regularly forced to sell property to pay the taxes, reducing the value of the inheritance. Not until the Taxpayer Relief Act of 1997 was the tax exclusion set at a significant amount ($625,000). See Harvey J. Platt, *Your Living Trust and Estate Plan*, 3rd ed. (New York: Allworth Press, 2002), pp. 94–107.

3. For example, dependents and survivor's benefits were added in 1939, disability insurance benefits were added in 1956, and early retirement benefits were added in 1961.

4. Stephen J. Entin, "Reducing the Social Security Benefits Tax," National Center for Policy Analysis, NCPA Brief Analysis No. 332, August 10, 2000.

5. Entin, "Reducing the Social Security Benefits Tax." Technically, these thresholds refer to "modified gross income," which is defined as all ordinary adjusted gross income, plus half of Social Security benefits, plus income from tax-exempt bonds.

6. Entin, "Reducing the Social Security Benefits Tax."

7. Note, however, that today's young people will pay more in Social Security taxes than they will ever receive in benefits. See Laurence J. Kotlikoff, "Privatizing Social Security," National Center for Policy Analysis, NCPA Policy Report No. 217, July 1998.

8. This section is largely based on Bruce Bartlett, "Wealth, Mobility, Inheritance and the Estate Tax," National Center for Policy Analysis, NCPA Policy Report No. 235, July 2000.

9. Richard F. Fullenbaum and Mariana A. McNeil, *The Effects of the Federal Estate and Gift Tax on the Aggregate Economy*, Working Paper No. 98-01 (Washington, D.C.: Research Institute for Small and Emerging Business, 1998).

10. Bartlett, "Wealth, Mobility, Inheritance and the Estate Tax," p. 10. Only Japan has higher estate taxes than the United States.

11. Martin A. Sullivan, "For Richest Americans, Two-Thirds of Wealth Escapes Estate Tax," Tax Notes, vol. 87, April 17, 2000, pp. 328–33.

12. George Cooper, *A Voluntary Tax? New Perspectives on Sophisticated Estate Tax Avoidance* (Washington, D.C.: Brookings Institution, 1979), p. 4.

13. Henry J. Aaron and Alicia H. Munnell, "Reassessing the Role for Wealth Transfer Taxes," *National Tax Journal*, vol. 45, June 1992, p. 130.

14. *Health Care Financing Review: Medicare and Medicaid Statistical Supplement*, HCFA Pub. No. 03417, November 1999.

15. Sandra Christensen and Judy Shinogle, "Effects of Supplemental Coverage on Use of Service by Medicare Enrollees," *Health Care Financing Review*, Fall 1997. Most studies find the increased spending is due to the perverse incentives of insurance and not because the patients were sicker. For a discussion, see Susan L. Ettner, "Adverse Selection and the Purchase of Medigap Insurance by the Elderly," *Journal of Health Economics*, vol. 16, no. 5, October 1, 1997, pp. 543–62; and Michael D. Hurd and Kathleen McGarry, "Medical Insurance and the Use of Health Care Services by Elderly," *Journal of Health Economics*, vol. 16, no. 2, April 1997, pp. 129–54.

16. Mark E. Litow, "Defined Contributions as an Option in Medicare," National Center for Policy Analysis, Policy Report No. 231, February 2000. This report is summarized in John C. Goodman and Sean R. Tuffnell, "Prescription Drugs and Medicare Reform," National Center for Policy Analysis, NCPA Brief Analysis No. 314, March 16, 2000.

17. Howard Gleckman, "Commentary: This Medicare Reform Is No Cure," *Business Week*, July 14, 2003.

18. "The Myth of Unaffordability: How Most Americans Should, Could, and Would Buy Private Long-Term Care Insurance," Center for Long-Term Care Financing, September 1, 1999.

19. MetLife, "The MetLife Market Survey of Nursing Home and Home Care Costs," August 2003.

20. "LTC Choice: A Simple, Cost-Free Solution to the Long-Term Care Financing Puzzle," Center for Long-Term Care Financing, September 1, 1998.

21. Two trillion dollars is 31 million Medicare enrollees times an average cost of $66,000 per year for a nursing home stay. "Nursing Home Costs Average $181 Per Day in U.S.," MetLife, August 5, 2003.

22. Bush supported a tax exemption of $3,000 in 2002 for persons who take care of parents or children needing long-term assistance, allowing taxpayers to deduct 100 percent of the cost of private long-term care insurance, and the expansion of medical savings accounts. See Richard L. Clarke, "It's Bush. Now What?" *Health Care Financial Management*, January 2001; and "Fact Sheet: President Outlines Agenda for Improving Health Security in the Best Health Care System in the World," Office of the Press Secretary, The White House, February 11, 2002.

23. Most funded long-term care services in this country are provided by Medicaid under the "medical model," where physicians and nurses supervise health-care workers providing medical services. However, consumer-directed personal assistance services are growing in popularity under what is known as the "independent living model" of long-term care. See Andrew I. Batavia, "A Right to Personal Assistance Services: 'Most Integrated Setting Appropriate' Requirements and the Independent Living Model of Long-Term Care," *American Journal of Law & Medicine*, Spring 2001; and Keren Brown Wilson, "An Aging America Faces the Assisted Living Alternative," *USA Today*, March 2000.

# CHAPTER 10

1. "Social Security: A Primer," Congressional Budget Office, September 2001.

2. This assumes net immigration is zero and constant death rates. To keep the population at its current size each woman must have an average of two children to replace one adult male and one adult female. (The additional 0.1 makes up for children who do not live to adulthood.)

3. Estimates of the tax burden for Social Security and Medicare Parts A and B are taken from the 2001 National Center for Policy Analysis calculations and *2001 Annual Report of the Board of Trustees of the Federal Old-Age and*

*Survivors Insurance and Disability Insurance Trust Funds.* Estimates for the burden of other health spending were made by the National Center for Policy Analysis.

4. At that time, the normal retirement age will be 67.

5. John C. Goodman and Matt Moore, "Government Spending on the Elderly: Social Security and Medicare," National Center for Policy Analysis, NCPA Policy Report No. 247, November 2001, p. 23.

6. See Matt Moore, "Two Cheers for the Commission to Strengthen Social Security," National Center for Policy Analysis, NCPA Brief Analysis No. 387, December 18, 2001.

7. See John C. Goodman, "Social Security Reform: The NCPA's 'Hybrid' Plan," National Center for Policy Analysis, NCPA Brief Analysis No. 385, December 8, 2001.

8. Bill McInturff and Matt Moore, "Americans Support Personal Retirement Accounts," National Center for Policy Analysis, NCPA Brief Analysis No. 333, August 14, 2000.

9. Melissa Hieger and William Shipman, "Common Objections to a Market Based Social Security System: A Response," Cato Institute, SSP No. 10, July 22, 1997, p. 9.

10. John C. Goodman, "Administering Private Social Security Accounts," National Center for Policy Analysis, NCPA Brief Analysis No. 289, April 20, 1999.

11. Estelle James, Alejandra Cox Edwards, and Rebeca Wong, "The Impact of Social Security Reform on Women in Three Countries," NCPA Policy Report No. 264, November 4, 2003.

12. Goodman, "Social Security Reform: The NCPA's 'Hybrid' Plan."

## CHAPTER 11

1. Oshanette's story is taken from a newspaper profile. Tina Griego, "Life After Welfare Tiring but Fulfilling," *Rocky Mountain News*, September 6, 2003.

2. John C. Goodman, "Taxpayer Choice: A Common Sense Solution to the Crisis of the Welfare State," Issue Analysis Report No. 4, July 1995, Goldwater Institute.

3. National Center for Health Statistics, Centers for Disease Control.

4. John C. Goodman, Gerald W. Reed, and Peter S. Ferrara, "Why Not Abolish the Welfare State?" National Center for Policy Analysis, NCPA Policy Report No. 187, October 1994, p. 3.

5. *Economic Report of the President* (Washington, D.C.: U.S. Government Printing Office, 1989).

6. Goodman, Reed, and Ferrara, "Why Not Abolish the Welfare State?" p. 6.

7. "Consumer Expenditures in 1999," May 2001, Bureau of Statistics, U.S. Department of Labor, table 1.

8. Robert Rector, Kate Walsh O'Beirne, and Michael McLaughlin, "How 'Poor' Are America's Poor?" Heritage Backgrounder No. 791, September 21, 1990; and Robert Rector, "How the Poor Really Live: Lessons for Welfare Reform," Heritage Backgrounder No. 875, January 31, 1992, pp. 12–13.

9. Bernard D. Karpinos, *Height and Weight of Military Youths* (Medical Statistics Division, Office of the Surgeon General, U.S. Department of the Army, 1960), pp. 336–51.

10. Bureau of the Census, *Characteristics of Households and Persons Receiving Selected Noncash Benefits, 1983* (Washington, D.C.: U.S. Department of Commerce, 1985), series P-60, no. 148, pp. 1–5, 103.

11. Daniel N. Shapiro, "Effective Marginal Tax Rates on Low-Income Households," Employment Policies Institute, February 1999.

12. Mary Jo Bane and David T. Ellwood, *Welfare Realities: From Rhetoric to Reform* (Cambridge, Mass.: Harvard University Press, 1994), pp. 30–36.

13. Bane and Ellwood, *Welfare Realities*, p. 31.

14. Bane and Ellwood, *Welfare Realities*, p. 39.

15. Bane and Ellwood, *Welfare Realities*, p. 49.

16. Interviews with Texas Department of Human Services administrators and Dallas Salvation Army personnel. Reported in Goodman and Stroup, "Privatizing the Welfare State," National Center for Policy Analysis, NCPA Policy Report No. 123, June 1996, pp. 23–24.

17. Martin Rein and Lee Rainwater, "Patterns of Welfare Use," *Social Service Review*, no. 52, pp. 511–34, cited in Greg Duncan, *Years of Poverty, Years of Plenty* (Ann Arbor, Mich.: Institute for Social Research, 1984), p. 78.

18. Burton A. Abrams and Mark D. Schmitz, "The Crowding-Out Effect of Governmental Transfers on Private Charitable Contributions: Cross Section Evidence," National Tax Journal, 1984, no. 4, table I, p. 564. For discussion of various estimates of this effect, see Eric J. Brunner, "An Empirical Test of Neutrality and the Crowding-out Hypothesis," Public Choice, 1997, Nos. 3–4, pp. 261–79.

19. Goodman, Reed, and Ferrara, "Why Not Abolish the Welfare State?" p. 26.

20. Sheila Zedleuashi et al., "Potential Effects of Congressional Welfare Reform Legislation on Family Incomes," Urban Institute, table 3, July 26, 1996.

21. Katha Pollitt, "What We Know," *New Republic*, August 1996.

22. June E. O'Neill and M. Anne Hill, "Gaining Ground: Women, Welfare Reform and Work," National Center for Policy Analysis, NCPA Policy Report No. 251, February 2002.

23. O'Neill and Hill, "Gaining Ground."

24. O'Neill and Hill, "Gaining Ground."

25. Statement by Tommy G. Thompson, secretary, Department of Health and Human Services, before the Committee on Ways and Means, U. S. House of Representatives, March 12, 2002.

26. Joe Loconte, "God, Government and the Good Samaritans," *Compassion and Culture*, Capital Research Center, March 2002, and Heritage Foundation, 2001.

27. Press Release, "Total Giving Reaches $203.45 Billion As Charitable Contributions Increase 6.6 Percent in 2000," May 23, 2001, AAFRC Trust for Philanthropy.

28. John C. Goodman, "Taxpayer Choice," National Center for Policy Analysis, Brief Analysis No. 206, June 1996.

29. Clint Bolick, "Are School Vouchers Constitutional?" National Center for Policy Analysis, NCPA Brief Analysis No. 272, July 10, 1998.

# INDEX

~

# About the Authors

~

**Kimberley A. Strassel** is a senior editorial page writer for *The Wall Street Journal*. She joined the editorial page in 1999, after working as a news reporter for Dow Jones in London and New York. Ms. Strassel is a native of Oregon and a graduate of Princeton University.

**Celeste Colgan** is an educational consultant and member of the National Council on the Humanities and the Board of Trustees of Mesa State College in Colorado. She formerly served as a senior fellow and director of the Women in the Economy Project of the National Center for Policy Analysis. Before joining the NCPA, she held various positions, including director of the Wyoming Department of Commerce, as a member of the faculty of the University of Wyoming and Casper College, and in corporate and family-owned businesses. Dr. Colgan received her Ph.D. from the University of Maryland, College Park.

**John C. Goodman** is founder and president of the National Center for Policy Analysis, a nonprofit public policy institute with offices in Dallas, Texas, and Washington, D.C. He is the author or coauthor of more than 200 articles and eight books, including *Lives at Risk* (2004). He received the prestigious Duncan Black Award for the best scholarly article on public choice economics in 1988. Dr. Goodman received a Ph.D. in economics from Columbia University and has taught at a number of colleges and universities.